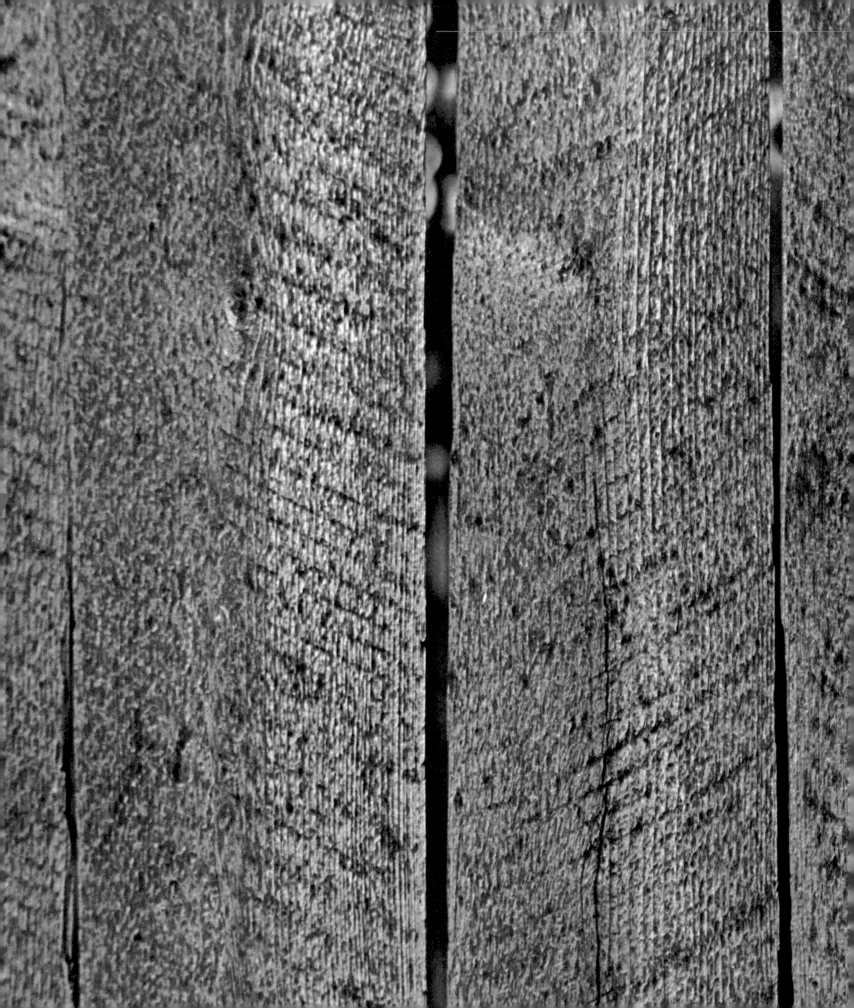

THE FAMILY
CREATIVE WORKSHOP

21

Traditional Knitting Motifs
Trapunto, Tree Houses
Treen Ware, Trellises, Tropical Fish
Tying Flies, Upholstery
Valentines, Vegetable Dyes

Plenary Publications International, Inc.
New York and Amsterdam

Published by Plenary Publications International, Incorporated 300 East 40th Street, New York, N. Y., 10016, for the Blue Mountain Crafts Council.

Library of Congress Catalog Card Number: 73-89331. Complete set International Standard Book Number: 0-88459-021-6. Volume 21 International Standard Book Number: 0-88459-020-8

Manufactured in the United States of America. Printed and bound by the W. A. Krueger Company, Brookfield, Wisconsin.

Printing preparation by Lanman Lithoplate Company.

Publishers:
Plenary Publications International, Incorporated 300 East 40th Street New York, New York 10016

Steven R. Schepp
EDITOR-IN-CHIEF

Jerry Curcio
PRODUCTION MANAGER

Jo Springer
VOLUME EDITOR

Joanne Delaney
Ellen Foley
EDITORIAL ASSISTANTS

Editorial preparation:
Tree Communications, Inc. 250 Park Avenue South New York, New York 10003

Rodney Friedman
EDITORIAL DIRECTOR

Ronald Gross
DESIGN DIRECTOR

Paul Levin
DIRECTOR OF PHOTOGRAPHY

Jill Munves
TEXT EDITOR

Sonja Douglas
ART DIRECTOR

Rochelle Lapidus
Marsha Gold
DESIGNERS

Lucille O'Brien
EDITORIAL PRODUCTION

Ruth Forst Michel
COPYREADER

Eva Gold
ADMINISTRATIVE MANAGER

Editors for this volume:
Andrea DiNoto
UPHOLSTERY

Donal Dinwiddie
TREEN
TRELLISES

Michael Donner
TREE HOUSES
VEGETABLE DYES

Rodney Friedman
TYING FLIES

Linda Hetzer
TRAPUNTO
VALENTINES

Marilyn Nierenberg
TROPICAL FISH

Mary Grace Skurka
TRADITIONAL KNITTING MOTIFS

Originating editor of the series:
Allen Davenport Bragdon

Contributing editors:
Wendy Murphy
Dennis Starin

Contributing illustrators:
Marina Givotovsky
Patricia Lee
Lynn Matus
Sally Shimizu

Contributing photographers:
Steven Mays
Dennis Starin

Production:
Thom Augusta
Phil Gim
Christopher Jones
Patricia Lee
Alan Okada
Leslie Strong
Gregory Wong

Photo and illustration credits:
TRAPUNTO: Photograph, page 2581, courtesy of the Smithsonian Institution. TREE HOUSES: Engraving of tree-house restaurant, page 2592, courtesy of Photo Harlingue-Viollet, Paris. TROPICAL FISH: Photographs of tropical fish, pages 2626, 2638, and 2639, courtesy of Walter Johanson, The Studio, New York, N. Y.

Acknowledgement:
The editors thank the Aquarium Stock Company, Inc., New York, N. Y. for guidance and cooperation.

The Project-Evaluation Symbols appearing in the title heading at the beginning of each project have these meanings:

Range of approximate cost:
¢ Low: under $5 or free and found natural materials
$ Medium: about $10
$$ High: above $15

Estimated time to completion for an unskilled adult:
Hours
Days
Weeks

Suggested level of experience:
Child alone
Supervised child or family project
Unskilled adult
Specialized prior training

Tools and equipment:
Small hand tools
Large hand and household tools
Specialized or powered equipment

On the cover:
Fishermen make artificial flies of bits of fur and feathers tied with thread to a fishing hook. Materials displayed are golden-pheasant-crest tippet, Plymouth-Rock-hen hackle, brown hackle, black mohair, and ginger deer hair along with a No. 8 wet-fly hook and a bobbin of tying thread. Photograph by Paul Levin.

**Contents and
craftspeople for Volume 21:**

Folk Art You Can Wear

Helen Maris was a painter and sculptor when she traded her paints, brushes, and chisels for yarn and knitting needles to explore knitting as an art form. She knits for several fashion designers and her work has been pictured in many magazines and yarn-company publications. A native of Steubenville, Ohio, Helen studied at Carnegie-Mellon University in Pittsburgh and at the Art Students League in New York, where she lives.

Through the ages in every culture, people have used symbols to decorate buildings, furniture, utensils, and clothing. Some symbols were derived from religious beliefs, others signified the power and prestige of the owner, or imitated nature, or were simply the expression of a need for beauty in everyday life. Because knitting was one of the ancient handcrafts, these symbols appeared on the knitted garments of everyone from high priest to peasant. Some of the traditional designs that have survived remain just as they were centuries ago; others have been modified by so many knitters that the original meanings—though not the beauty of the patterns—are lost.

Many of these time-tested knitting motifs use a variety of colors (opposite and below); others derive their impact from texture alone. Perhaps the most sophisticated in the use of color are the Fair Isle patterns (the island is one of the Shetland Islands off the coast of northern Scotland). In these, background colors are changed as often as design colors. Scandinavian motifs are notable for representations of nature in crisp, cheerful color combinations. Fishermen and sailors of the British Isles, who produced beautiful knitting at one time, represented the ropes, fishing nets, and anchors of their trade in the designs of their sweaters. Shetland ring shawls were so called because the knit lace was so fine and cobwebby that a shawl could be pulled through a wedding ring. These designs are all part of a legacy of ideas for the creative knitter.

However, you needn't feel limited to traditional designs found only in the knitting of another era. You can also find knitting ideas in the traditional designs of oriental carpets, textiles from South America and Africa, American Indian blankets, Scandinavian wood carvings, Dutch tiles, even Etruscan pottery. You need only graph paper and a knowledge of basic knitting stitches to translate such designs into knitting motifs traditional in origin but ideal for contemporary use.

These colorful charts for traditional knitting designs only hint at the variety of representational and abstract motifs that can be adopted from cultures around the world. Other traditional knitting patterns, such as Irish-fisherman cables and knit laces, are based on texture rather than on color. For one version of the Irish-fisherman knit, see page 2571.

Fair Isle star motif

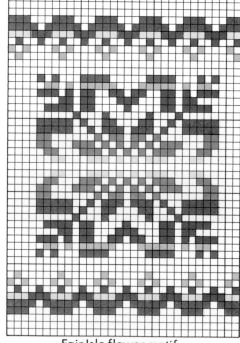

Fair Isle flower motif

British Isles motif

German motif

Universal motif

Albanian design

Argyle plaid

Scandinavian design

Dutch tile design

Bulgarian design

Scandinavian design

Fair Isle Tree-of-Life motif

Fair Isle Crown-of-Glory motif

2567

Abbreviations

psso	Pass slipped stitch over
MC	Main color
rnd	Round
st (s)	Stitch (es)
() or []	Repeat instructions enclosed by parentheses or brackets the number of times indicated.

Other abbreviations are given in parentheses under the illustrations.

Casting on with one needle

1. Make a slip knot around the needle, at a distance from the end of the yarn of about an inch for each stitch to be cast on.

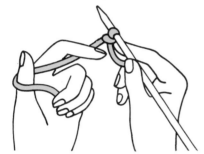

2. Hold the needle with the slip knot in your right hand and loop the length of yarn not attached to the ball around your left thumb.

3. Put the point of the needle under the loop on your left thumb, and put the yarn from the ball over the forefinger of your right hand.

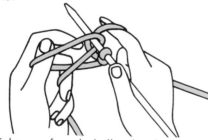

4. Take yarn from the ball under, then over the needle and through the loop made earlier, leaving the stitch on the needle.

5. Pull stitch on needle tight and bring yarn around thumb, ready for the next stitch. Repeat steps until the desired number of stitches are cast on. Switch the needle to left hand in preparation for knitting.

Knit stitch (K)

1. Hold needle with stitches in your left hand and the other needle in your right hand. Put the right needle through a stitch on the left needle from front to back. Take the yarn around the point of the right needle to make a loop.

2. Draw this new loop through the stitch on left needle, moving it to right needle.

3. Slip the stitch completely off the left needle.

Repeat these steps until you have pulled loops through all the stitches on the left needle and onto the right one.

To knit the next row, move the needle now holding stitches to your left hand and the empty needle to your right hand.

Purl stitch (P)

1. Hold needle filled with stitches in your left hand and the other needle in your right hand. Put the right needle through the stitch on the left needle from back to front, instead of front to back. Take the yarn around the point of the right needle to make a loop.

2. Pull this new loop through the stitch on the left needle, moving it to the right needle.

3. Slip the stitch completely off the left needle.

Repeat these steps until you have pulled loops through all the stitches on the left needle and onto the right one.

To work the next row, move the needle holding stitches to your left hand.

Increasing (inc)

The simplest way to make an extra stitch is to knit or purl the stitch in the usual manner, but do not slip it off the left needle. Instead, insert the right needle into the back of the stitch and knit into the stitch a second time. (To make an increase in a purl stitch, insert the needle through the front of the stitch.) Slip both stitches onto the right needle. You have made 2 stitches from 1 stitch.

KNITTING STITCHES

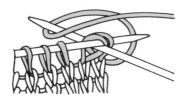

Decreasing (dec)

To decrease 1 stitch (K2 tog or P2 tog), insert the right needle through 2 stitches on the left needle, instead of the usual 1 and knit or purl them together.

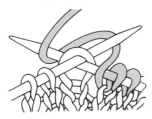

Yarn over—knit (yo)

To make a yarn over when knitting, bring yarn under the right needle to front of work, then over the needle to back, ready to knit the next stitch.

Yarn over—purl (yo)

To make a yarn over when purling, bring yarn over the right needle to back of work, then under the needle to front, ready to purl the next stitch.

To slip a stitch (sl st)

Insert the right needle into stitch as if to purl the stitch (unless directions read "as if to knit") and slip the stitch onto the right needle without working, being careful not to twist it.

To tie on a new strand of yarn

Join a new ball of yarn or a new color at the beginning of a row on straight needles by making a slip knot with the new strand around the working strand. Move the knot up to edge of work and continue with new ball. On circular needles, leave 4-inch tails on the old and the new yarn, and weave them into the back of the knitting in opposite directions.

Stranding colors

When two colors appear in the same row of a knitting pattern, the yarns are stranded, or floated, across the back of the work. To avoid the tangling and twisting caused by dropping one color and picking up the other, the

knitting can be done simultaneously with both colors, using a combination of the English and Continental methods of knitting. (With the English method, shown on the opposite page, the yarn is controlled by the right hand and three movements are needed to make a stitch; with the Continental method, the yarn is controlled by the left hand and only two movements—similar to those of crocheting—are used to make a stitch.) The yarn carried by the right hand should be the dominant color of the row, usually the main color of the pattern. Check the color chart before starting each row to determine this.

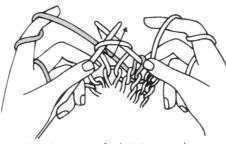

The hand positions for knitting are shown above. The arrow shows the movement of the right-hand needle in forming the stitch in the Continental manner.

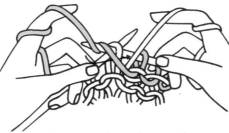

The hand positions for purling are shown above. The arrow shows the movement of the right-hand needle in forming the stitch in the Continental manner.

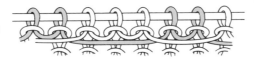

The back of the work done with the stranding technique looks like this. The floating yarn should not be pulled tight or the design on the front might be distorted.

Work even

Work in the same stitch or color pattern without increasing or decreasing.

Stockinette stitch (s st)

Knit 1 row, purl 1 row. On circular or double-pointed needles, knit every round.

Garter stitch (g st)

Knit every row. On circular or double-pointed needles, knit 1 round, purl 1 round. Two rows equal one ridge.

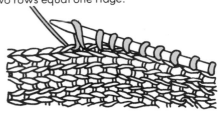

To pick up stitches along an edge

To add a border along the neckline of a sweater, you will need to pick up, rather than cast on, the new stitches. Hold right side facing you, with edge where stitches will be added at top. Insert needle between first and second stitches and wrap new yarn around needle. Draw yarn through loop and keep on right needle for first stitch. Work this way all around.

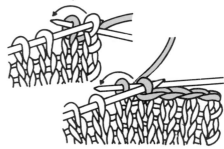

Binding off

Work 2 stitches in pattern loosely. With left needle, lift the first stitch over the second stitch and off the right needle. This is 1 stitch bound off. Work next stitch and repeat process. To bind off 6 stitches at the beginning of a row, you will work 7 stitches but the last stitch will remain on the right needle as the first stitch of the remainder of the row. To bind off a complete row, continue until all stitches but 1 are bound off. Break yarn and draw the yarn end through the stitch, forming a loose knot.

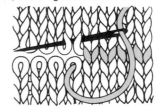

Weaving

To weave 2 edges of stockinette stitch together, work on the right side with a yarn needle and a length of matching yarn about 3 or 4 times as long as the rows to be woven. Follow the illustration to form new knit stitches between the rows for an invisible finish.

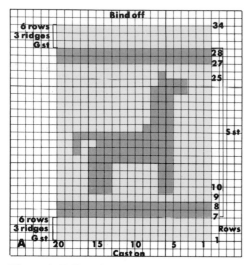

Figure A: Follow this chart to knit the llama design, starting at the lower right corner. In the stockinette-stitch section in the center of the chart, encompassing the llama image, read the knit rows from right to left and the purl rows from left to right.

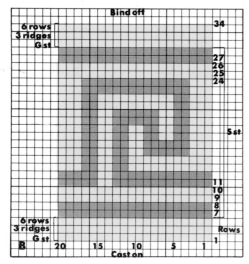

Figure B: Follow this chart to knit the Greek-key design, starting at the lower right corner. In the stockinette-stitch section in the center of the chart, read the knit rows from right to left, and the purl rows from left to right.

A llama, native to the South American Andes, is a traditional motif among Peruvian knitters; here one decorates a bulky-yarn tote bag.

On the other side of the tote bag, a classic Greek-key design, knitted in the same bright colors, has a very contemporary look.

Needlecrafts
Two-color shoulder bag

The brightly colored tote bag shown above, simple enough for a young knitter, is a good introduction to working with two colors. One side has a llama design, a common motif in Peruvian knitting. The Peruvians usually worked with yarns of natural colors—shades of beige, brown, off-white, gray, and black—from the alpaca, a close relative of the native llama. The other side of the tote has a Greek-key motif; it dates from antiquity but has a contemporary geometric look.

Materials: Bulky acrylic-and-nylon yarn, 1 skein each of purple and green (or more traditional colors if you like); one pair of No. 13 straight knitting needles; a large tapestry needle.
Size: The bag is approximately 8 by 9 inches.
Gauge: 2½ sts = 1 inch.

Directions for side with llama design
With green and No. 13 needles, cast on 20 sts.
Rows 1 through 6 (3 ridges): Work in g st (K every row).
Rows 7 and 8: With purple, K 1 row, P 1 row.
Row 9: With green, K across.
Rows 10 through 25: Work in s st (K odd-numbered rows, P even-numbered rows), following the two-color chart in Figure A. (Twist the unused color around the working color every 4th st to avoid long loops on the wrong side.)
Row 26: With green, P across.
Rows 27 and 28: With purple, K 1 row, P 1 row.

Rows 29 through 34 (3 ridges): With green, work in g st (K every row). Bind off loosely.

Directions for side with Greek key design
Work same as llama side through row 9.
Row 10: With green, P across.
Rows 11 through 24: Work in s st (K odd-numbered rows, P even-numbered rows), following the two-color chart in Figure B. (Twist the unused color around the working color every 4th st to avoid long loops on the wrong side.)
Rows 25 and 26: With green, K 1 row, P 1 row.
Rows 27 through 34: Work same as llama side. Bind off loosely.
Finishing: Sew side and bottom edges with green yarn and a large tapestry needle. Take 4 strands of green and 2 strands of purple, divide evenly into 3 sections, and braid together for the shoulder strap. Make it approximately 40 inches long, with 3 inches of yarn unbraided at each end. Knot the ends through the top row of stitches at the corners and let the ends hang free.

The sleeveless top is knit in one piece from border to border; the side-cable panels form the shoulder straps. Side edges are simply laced together with yarn—no sewing is required.

This toddler-sized cotton version of an Irish-fisherman knit can be layered over a shirt or sweater, or it can be worn by itself as a warm-weather tank top.

Needlecrafts
Child's Irish-knit top

Soft cotton yarn is used to make a toddler's tank-top (above) that is lightweight, comfortable, and washable. The size can easily be enlarged by adding complete cable panels or repeats, keeping an odd number of stitches in each seed-stitch side panel. The pattern is a combination of twisted cables with bobbles, a center braid cable, and side panels of seed stitch. The panels are separated by narrow panels of stockinette stitch and hemmed with garter-stitch borders.

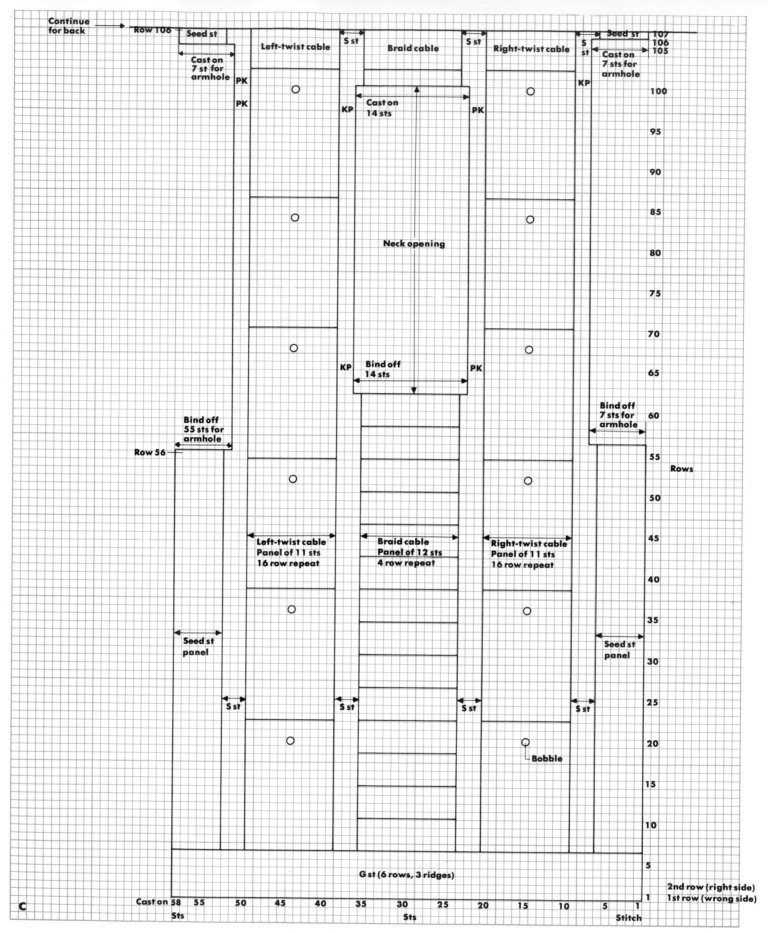

Figure C: This chart shows the shape of the child's Irish-knit tank top, worked in one flat piece, from the lower border on the front to the first 7 rows of the back.

Size: Child's size 2.

Materials: Three skeins of Lily's Sugar 'n Cream 4-ply, 100 percent cotton yarn (eggshell). One pair of No. 6 straight knitting needles. One small cable needle. Two stitch holders.

Gauge (in pattern): 4 sts = 1 inch; 6 rows = 1 inch.

Directions for front:

With No. 6 needles, cast on 58 sts.

Row 1 through 6 (border); Work in g st (3 ridges).

Row 7 (wrong side): (P1, K1) 3 times; P3; *left-twist cable*—K2, P7, K2; P3; *braid cable*—K2, P8, K2; P3; *right-twist cable*—K2, P7, K2, P3; (K1, P1) 3 times.

Row 8 (right side): (P1, K1) 3 times; K3; *right-twist cable*—P2, sl 3 sts to cable needle and hold in back, K4, K3 from cable needle, P2; K3; *braid cable*—P2, (sl 2 sts to cable needle) twice, P2; K3; *left-twist cable*—P2, sl 4 sts to cable needle and hold in front, K3, K4 from cable needle, P2; K3; (K1, P1) 3 times.

Row 9: Repeat row 7.

Row 10: (P1, K1) 3 times; K3; *right-twist cable*—P2, K7, P2, K3; *braid cable*—P2, K2, sl 2 sts to cable needle and hold in front, K2, K2 from cable needle, K2, P2, K3; *left-twist cable*—P2, K7, P2, K3; (K1, P1) 3 times.

Row 11: Repeat row 7.

Row 12: (P1, K1) 3 times; K3; *right-twist cable*—P2, K7, P2; K3; *braid cable*—P2, (sl 2 sts to cable needle and hold in back, K2, K2 from cable needle twice, P2, K2, P2; K3; (K1, P1) 3 times.

Row 13: Repeat row 7.

Row 14: (P1, K1) 3 times; K3; *right-twist cable*—P2, sl 3 sts to cable needle and hold in back, K4, K3 from cable needle, P2; K3; *braid cable*—P2, K2, sl 2 sts to cable needle and hold in front, K2, K2 from cable needle, K2, P2; K3; *left-twist cable*—P2, sl 4 sts to cable needle and hold in front, K3, K4 from cable needle, P2; K3; (K1, P1) 3 times.

Row 15: Repeat row 7.

Row 16: Repeat row 12.

Row 17: Repeat row 7.

Row 18: Repeat row 10.

Row 19: Repeat row 7.

Row 20: (P1, K1) 3 times; K3; *right-twist cable*—P2, K3, make bobble in center st as follows: [(K1, yo, K1, yo, K1) in same st, making 5 sts from 1 st; turn and K5; turn and P5; turn and sl 1, K1, psso, K1,

K2 tog; turn and P3 tog, completing bobble], K3, P2; K3; *braid cable*—P2, (sl 2 sts to cable needle and hold in back, K2, K2 from cable needle) twice, P2; K3; *left-twist cable*—P2, K3, make bobble in center st as before, K3, P2; K3.

Row 21: Repeat row 7.

Row 22: Repeat row 10.

Row 23: Repeat row 7.

Row 24: Repeat row 8.

Row 25: Repeat row 7.

Row 26: Repeat row 10.

Row 27: Repeat row 7.

Row 28: Repeat row 12.

Row 29: Repeat row 7.

Row 30: Repeat row 14.

Row 31: Repeat row 7.

Row 32: Repeat row 12.

Row 33: Repeat row 7.

Row 34: Repeat row 10.

Row 35: Repeat row 7.

Row 36: Repeat row 20.

Row 37: Repeat row 7.

Row 38: Repeat row 10.

Row 39: Repeat row 7.

Row 40: Repeat row 8.

Row 41: Repeat row 7.

Row 42: Repeat row 10.

Row 43: Repeat row 7.

Row 44: Repeat row 12.

Row 45: Repeat row 7.

Row 46: Repeat row 14.

Row 47: Repeat row 7.

Row 48: Repeat row 12.

Row 49: Repeat row 7.

Row 50: Repeat row 10.

Row 51: Repeat row 7.

Row 52: Repeat row 20.

Row 53: Repeat row 7.

Row 54: Repeat row 10.

Underarm shaping

Row 55: Bind off 7 sts; repeat row 7 from the next st.

Row 56: Bind off 7 sts; repeat row 8 from the next st to the next to the last st; P the last st.

Row 57: K1, P1; *left-twist cable*—K2, P7, K2; P3; *braid cable*—K2, P8, K2; P3; *right-twist cable*—K2, P7, K2; P1, K1.

Row 58: P1; K1; *right-twist cable*—P2, K7, P2; K3; *braid cable*—P2, K2, sl

2 sts to cable needle and hold in front, K2, K2 from cable needle, K2, P2; K3; *left-twist cable*—P2, K7, P2; K1, P1.

Row 59: Repeat row 57.

Row 60: P1, K1; *right-twist cable*—P2, K7, P2; K3, *braid cable*—P2, (sl 2 sts to cable needle and hold in back, K2, K2 from cable needle) twice, P2; K3; *left-twist cable*—P2, K7, P2; K1, P1.

Row 61: Repeat row 57.

Straps and neckline shaping

Row 62: P1, K1; *right-twist cable*—P2, sl 3 sts to cable needle and hold in back, K4, K3 from cable needle, P2; K1, P1. Put these 15 sts on stitch holder; they are the beginning of the right shoulder strap and will be worked later. Bind off 14 sts for neckline. K1; P2, sl 4 sts to cable needle and hold in front, K3, K4 from cable needle, P2; K1, P1. There should be 15 sts on needle; they are the beginning of the left shoulder strap.

Strap

Row 63: K1, P1; *left-twist cable*—K2, P7, K2; P1, K1.

Row 64: P1, K1; *left-twist cable*—P2, K7, P2; K1, P1.

Row 65: Repeat row 63.

Row 66: P1, K1; *left-twist cable*—P2, K7, P2; K1, P1.

Row 67: Repeat row 63.

Row 68: P1, K1; *left-twist cable*—P2, K3, make bobble in center st as before, K3, P2; K1, P1.

Row 69: Repeat row 63.

Row 70: Repeat row 66.

Row 71: Repeat row 63.

Row 72: P1, K1; *left-twist cable*—P2, sl 4 sts to cable needle and hold in front, K3, K4 from cable needle, P2; K1, P1.

Row 73: Repeat row 63.

Row 74: Repeat row 66.

Row 75: Repeat row 63.

Row 76: Repeat row 64.

Row 77: Repeat row 63.

Row 78: Repeat row 72.

Row 79: Repeat row 63.

Row 80: Repeat row 64.

Row 81: Repeat row 63.

Row 82: Repeat row 66.

Row 83: Repeat row 63.

Row 84: Repeat row 68.

Row 85: Repeat row 63.

Row 86: Repeat row 66.

2573

CRAFTNOTES: EMBROIDERY STITCHES

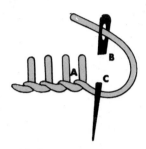

Blanket stitch
Work from left to right. Bring needle up at A. Loop yarn in position shown, insert needle at B with point coming up at C and the yarn looped under needle. Draw yarn through. Repeat B-C across.

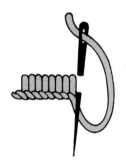

Buttonhole stitch
A closed blanket stitch. Proceed as for blanket stitch, but space stitches close together, as shown.

Row 87: Repeat row 63.
Row 88: Repeat row 72.
Row 89: Repeat row 63.
Row 90: Repeat row 66.
Row 91: Repeat row 63.
Row 92: Repeat row 64.
Row 93: Repeat row 63.
Row 94: Repeat row 78.
Row 95: Repeat row 63.
Row 96: Repeat row 64.
Row 97: Repeat row 63.
Row 98: Repeat row 66.
Row 99: Repeat row 63. Slip these 15 sts onto a stitch holder. Return to beginning of the right strap; transfer sts from holder to No. 6 needle. Attach yarn and knit row 63 (wrong side). Repeat rows 64 through 71.
Row 72: P1, K1; *right-twist cable*—P2, sl 3 sts to cable needle and hold in back, K4, K3 from cable needle, P2; K1, P1. Repeat rows 73 through 77.
Row 78: Repeat row 75.
Repeat rows 79 through 87.
Row 88: Repeat row 72.
Repeat rows 89 through 93.
Row 94: Repeat row 72.
Repeat rows 95 through 99.

Back (worked in one piece with the front and shoulder straps)

Row 100: Repeat row 68; then cast on 14 sts for neckline. Transfer 15 sts from holder to right-hand needle and join these left strap sts to cast-on neckline sts. Repeat row 100 for the left shoulder strap. There should be 44 sts on needle.
Row 101: Repeat row 57.
Row 102: Repeat row 58.
Row 103: Repeat row 57.
Row 104: P1, K1; *right-twist cable*—P2, sl 3 sts to cable needle and hold in back, K4, K3 from cable needle, P2; K3; *braid cable*—P2, (sl 2 sts to cable needle and hold in back, K2, K2 from cable needle) twice, P2; K3; *left-twist cable*—P2, sl 4 sts to cable needle and hold in front, K3, K4 from cable needle, P2; K1, P1.
Row 105: Repeat row 57. At the end of this row, cast on 7 sts (51 sts).
Row 106: (P1, K1) 3 times; K3; *right-twist cable*—P2, K7, P2; K3; *braid cable*—P2, K2, sl 2 sts to cable needle and hold in front, K2, K2 from cable needle, K2, P2; K3; *left-twist cable*—P2, K7, P2; K2. At the end of this row, cast on 7 sts (58 sts).
Row 107: Repeat row 7.
Rows 108 through 153: Repeat rows 12 through 57.
Rows 154 through 159: Work in g st. Bind off.

Finishing
Cut two strands of yarn approximately 45 inches long and lace one through each side opening from underarm to border. Tie ends in bows.

Working on the wrong side, embroider blanket st or buttonhole st across the 14 sts of front and back necklines (see Craftnotes, left).

Needlecrafts
Norwegian-pattern sweater $ 🧍 📇 🧨

As an example of how to adapt traditional motifs to suit current styles, consider the wraparound sweater shown opposite. The deep round-yoke effect is a typically Scandinavian design feature, but the pattern is knit with yarns of earthy colors on a light-grey background, rather than in the more typical bright colors on white. The yarn is from Icelandic sheep. The motifs are simple geometric shapes, repeated in an orderly fashion.

Materials: Reynolds Lopi, single ply, 100 percent Icelandic sheep wool: 6 skeins of No. 7356 Light Grey (MC); 2 skeins of No. 7357 Dark Grey (A); 1 skein each of No. 7352 Dark Brown (B), and No. 7366 Rust (C); No. 10 knitting needles: 24-inch, 29-inch, and 36-inch (optional) circular and 16-inch circular or four double-pointed.

Size: Women's size medium. For size small, work same as medium except note change in right front section.
Gauge: 3½ sts = 1 inch; 4 rows = 1 inch.

Directions for body of sweater
With 29-inch No. 10 circular needle and MC, cast on 95 sts; do not join.

In this wrap sweater with a Norwegian pattern, the same earth-tone design encircles the bottom of the sweater and the sleeves; a slightly different pattern creates the deep round-yoke effect.

Rows 1 (wrong side) through 6: Working back and forth as you would on straight needles, work in s st, starting with a P row.

Row 7: *P9, inc in next st, repeat from * across to last 5 sts, P4, inc in last st (105 sts on needle).

Row 8: (turning row): *K2 tog, yo, repeat from * across. This type of turning row is called a picot hem and gives a pretty, scalloped edging.

Rows 9 through 11: Work in s st, starting with a P row.

Rows 12 through 39: Work color pattern back and forth in s st, following chart in Figure D, page 2576.

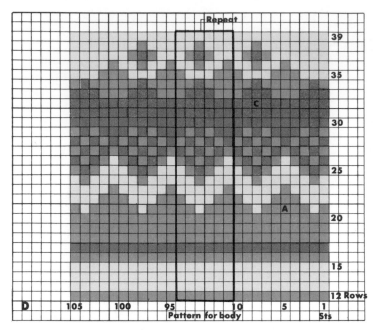

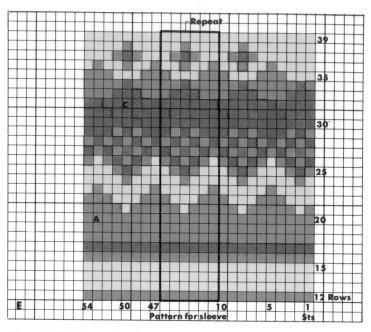

Figure D: This chart gives the pattern for the bottom of the wraparound sweater, from row 12 through row 39. Work the pattern in the section marked *repeat* from stitch 11 through stitch 94.

Figure E: This chart gives the pattern for the sleeve from row 12 through row 39. Work the pattern in the section marked *repeat* from stitch 11 through stitch 46.

Next, work even with MC for 8¾ inches (or desired length to underarm). Put body stitches on a length of yarn and begin work on the sleeves. (A length of yarn will hold more stitches and is more flexible than a large stitch holder.)

Sleeves (worked in the round)
With 24-inch No. 10 needles and MC, cast on 54 sts and join, being careful not to twist sts; mark beginning of rnd.

Rnds 1 through 7: K every rnd.

Rnd 8 (turning rnd): *K 2 tog, yo, repeat from * around.

Rnds 9 through 11: K every rnd.

Rnds 12 through 39: Work color pattern in s st (K every rnd), following the chart in Figure E. Note that the color pattern will break at the beginning of each rnd; this point will be considered the underarm seam when joining the sleeves to the body of the sweater.

Rnds 40 through 42: With MC, K.

Rnd 43: K12, K2 tog (mark this dec), K26, K2 tog (mark this dec), K12 (52 sts).

Work even, dec 1 st at each marker every 5th rnd, 6 times more (40 sts).

When the sleeve becomes too narrow to work on the 24-inch needle, switch to the 16-inch circular or four double-pointed needles.

Work even until length of sleeve is 17 inches (or desired length) from turning row. Put remaining 40 sts on length of yarn. Repeat for the other sleeve.

Yoke
The circular yoke design is worked across the body and the tops of the sleeves at the same time, joining them. To work the yoke, you must transfer all but the underarm stitches (to be woven together later) onto the same circular needle (Figure F).

Starting at one front edge of the body, transfer the first 14 sts from the yarn stitch holder onto a 29-inch or 36-inch No. 10 circular needle. Leave the next 13 body sts on the yarn (underarm). Transfer 27 sts of one sleeve to the needle, leaving the other 13 sts on the yarn (the break in the color pattern should be in center of this section). Transfer the next 55 sts from the body back onto the needle, repeat the sleeve directions for the second sleeve, and transfer the 14 sts remaining at the other front edge of the body (137 sts on the needle).

Rows 1 and 2: Working back and forth as you would on straight needles, work with MC in s st, starting with a K row.

Row 3: K, dec 3 sts evenly spaced across (134 sts on needle).

Rows 4 through 20: Work color pattern in s st, following the chart in Figure G.

Row 21: With B, *K1, K2 tog, repeat from * across to last 2 sts, K2 (90 sts).

Row 22: With A, P across.

Row 23: With A, K across.

Row 24: With MC, P across.

Row 25: With A, K across.

Row 26: With C, P across.

Row 27: With A, K across.

Row 28: With A, *K1, K2 tog, repeat from * across (60 sts).

Row 29 (switch to 24-inch needle): *With B, K1; with C, K1; repeat from * across.

Row 30: *With C, P1; with B, P1; repeat from * across.

Row 31: Repeat row 29.

Row 32: Repeat row 30.

Row 33: Repeat row 29.

Row 34: With A, P across.

Row 35: With MC, K across.

Row 36: With MC, P across.

Row 37: With A, K across.

Row 38: With A, *P1, P2 tog, repeat from * across (40 sts on needle).

Row 39: With A, K across.

Row 40: With A, *P3, P2 tog, repeat from * across (32 sts on needle).

Row 41: With A, K across.

Back neck shaping
To shape neck, work short rows back and forth, starting on the wrong side.

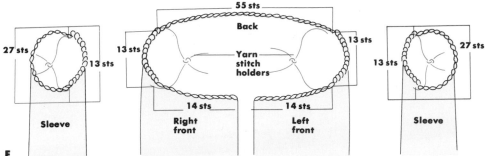

F

Figure F: The yoke design of the sweater is worked across the body and the tops of the sleeves at the same time. To join the three sections, transfer the first 14 stitches of each front, the 55 stitches of the back, and 27 stitches from each sleeve onto a No. 10 circular needle, in the proper sequence. Leave 13 stitches at the underarms of both the body and the sleeves on yarn stitch holders; weave together later.

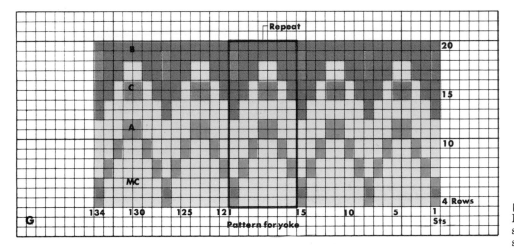

Figure G: This chart gives the yoke pattern from row 4 to row 20. Work the pattern in the section marked *repeat* from stitch 16 to stitch 120.

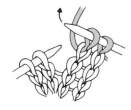

H

Figure H: To avoid holes at the turnings of the short rows used to shape the back neckline of the sweater, pick up a stitch from below the stitch just before the loose stitch and knit it together with the loose stitch.

Note: To avoid loose holes at the turning points, pick up a stitch from below the stitch just knit and work it together with the loose stitch (Figure H).

Row 1: P to within last 7 sts, turn.

Row 2: Sl 1, K to within last 7 sts, turn.

Row 3: Sl 1, P18 sts, turn.

Row 4: Sl 1, K20 sts, turn.

Row 5: Sl 1, P to end of row. Put remaining sts on length of yarn.

Hems

Before the front bands are worked, turn under the hems on the body of the sweater and on the sleeves at the turning row and sew.

Right front band

With 29-inch or 36-inch No. 10 circular needle and A, pick up 106 sts along the right-front edge of the body of the sweater. The band is g st (K every row).

Note: For size small, bind off after row 26, making the band about 2 inches narrower. Repeat for the left-front band.

Row 1: With A, *K9, K2 tog, repeat from * across to last 7 sts, K7 (97 sts).

Row 2: With A, K across (right side).

Row 3: With A, K across (wrong side).

Rows 4 and 5: With MC, K across.

Row 6: With A, *K9, K2 tog, repeat from * across to last 9 sts, K9 (89 sts).

Row 7: With A, K across.

Rows 8 and 9: With B, K across.

Rows 10 and 11: With C, K across.

Rows 12 and 13: With B, K across.

Rows 14 and 15: With C, K across.

Rows 16 and 17: With A, K across.

Rows 18 through 21: With MC, K.

Rows 22 and 23: With A, K across.

Rows 24 through 29: With MC, K.

Rows 30 through 33: With A, K across.

Rows 34 and 35: With MC, K across.

Rows 36 and 37: With A, K across.

Row 38: With MC, K across. Bind off loosely.

Left-front band

Work same as right-front band.

Neckline

Slip the back neck sts from the yarn to the 24-inch No. 10 circular needle. Then, with the wrong side of the sweater facing you and using the 29-inch or 36-inch No. 10 circular needle and color A, pick up and K20 sts along the top of the left-front band, K the back neck sts and pick up and K20 sts along the edge of the right-front band (75 sts).

Next: Work 4 rows in g st, 2 with A, then 2 with MC. Bind off loosely.

Finishing

Weave together the underarm stitches remaining on the lengths of yarn (Figure F).

Belt

With B, and No. 10 needles, cast on 7 sts. K15 rows. With C, K8 rows. With A, K4 rows. With MC, K for 45 inches. With A, K4 rows. With B, K8 rows. With C, K15 rows. Bind off loosely.

Figure I: The chart below shows how the scarf is knit on the diagonal. The knitting starts with only 3 stitches in one corner and increases are made until there are 51 stitches. To keep the shaping even throughout the length of the scarf, decreases are made on one edge and increases on the other edge. Decreases shape the other end. Although the ends look triangular in this working chart, they will square off in the actual knitting. Follow the chart for the color pattern; 1 square equals 1 stitch and 1 row of squares equals 1 row of stitches.

The bias-knit scarf is seamed lengthwise down the center back to form a tube. The scalloped edges are a result of the increases and decreases made along the edges to shape the scarf.

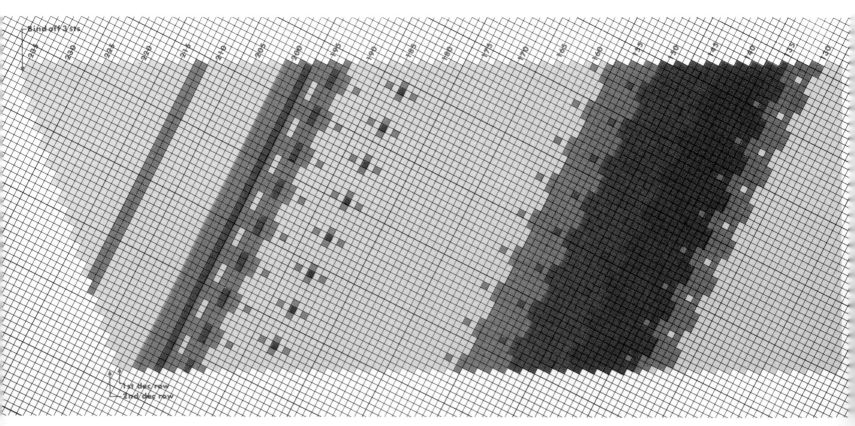

Needlecrafts
Bias-knit scarf

The pattern for the bias-knit scarf is coordinated with the patterns for the wrap-around sweater on page 2575.

Materials: Reynolds Lopi, single ply, 100 percent Icelandic sheep wool: 3 skeins of No. 7356 Light Grey (MC); and 1 skein each of No. 7357 Dark Grey (A); 7352 Dark Brown (B); and No. 7366 Rust (C); No. 10 straight or circular needles.

Size: Finished size of the scarf is about 63 inches long and 6 inches wide.

Gauge: 3½ sts = 1 inch; 4 rows = 1 inch.

Directions

With MC and No. 10 needles, cast on 3 sts.

Row 1 (wrong side): P across.

Row 2: Cast on 2 sts, K across to last 2 sts, inc in next st, K1.

Row 3: P across.

Rows 4 through 24: Repeat rows 2 and 3 until there are 39 sts on needle, ending with a K row.

Row 25: With A, repeat row 3.

Row 26: Repeat row 2 (42 sts on needle).

Rows 27 through 33: With MC, and starting with a P row, repeat rows 2 and 3 until there are 51 sts on needle, ending with a P row.

Row 34 (first shaping row): K1, K2 tog, K to last 2 sts, inc in next st, K1.

Row 35 (second shaping row): With A, P across.

Rows 36 through 203: Work color pattern, following the chart in Figure I. At the same time, repeat shaping rows 34 (on even-numbered rows) and 35 (on odd-numbered rows).

Row 204 (first decrease row): With MC, K1, K2 tog, K across to end *without* making an inc in the next to the last st (50 sts).

Row 205 (second decrease row): Bind off first 2 sts as to P, P across (48 sts).

Rows 206 through 211: With MC, repeat 2 decrease rows (204 and 205) until 39 sts remain.

Rows 212 and 213: With A, repeat 2 decrease rows (36 sts).

Rows 214 through 235: With MC, repeat 2 decrease rows (204 and 205) until 3 sts remain. Bind off as to K.

Finishing: Fold scarf lengthwise so that the edges meet in the center (the pattern will not meet at the seam). Sew with MC yarn and a tapestry needle. Block lightly.

For related projects, see "Knitting to Fit."

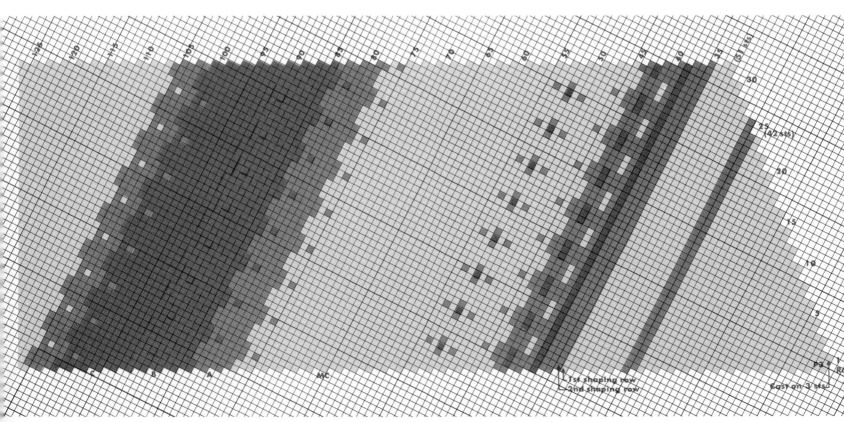

TRAPUNTO
Padded and Corded Quilting

Trapunto is a special kind of quilting in which parts of the design are given a sculptured look with a filling of polyester fiber, lamb's wool, cotton, or yarn. Also known as Italian quilting, trapunto can be worked in two ways. In the first method, called padded quilting, the design areas are outlined with stitching that joins a backing fabric to a top fabric. The backing is then slit with scissors, and the design pockets are stuffed. Then the slits are stitched closed. The design areas are kept small: large areas cannot be stuffed evenly. The second method is called corded quilting. In this case, the design stitched on the fabric consists of double lines spaced just far enough apart to accommodate the cording yarn. After the design is stitched, the backing is slit at intervals and yarn is threaded between the two rows of stitching.

The word trapunto comes from the Italian word for quilting. It is believed that this kind of quilting originated in Italy, perhaps because in the warm Mediterranean areas a full interlining of batting would be uncomfortable.

The techniques of cording and stuffing are very old. They were used in the oldest known bed quilt, made in Sicily in the late fourteenth century. The quilt was made of linen, with scenes from the legend of Tristan stitched in brown and white linen thread. The corded areas were threaded with wool.

In England in the seventeenth and eighteenth centuries, cording was used to decorate men's waistcoats, women's petticoats, baby clothing, and linen quilts. Often the fabric was so laden with cording that there was hardly any background space. The designs used most often depicted vases and baskets. Similar motifs appeared a century later in American quilts. A modern quilt with a basket motif is shown on page 2591. In America, cording was usually combined with stuffing. An American quilt with an intricate use of corded and stuffed work is *A Representation of the Fair Ground Near Russellville, Kentucky* (below). This white cotton quilt was made by Virginia Ivey in 1856 to commemorate a visit to the fair. It is now in the Smithsonian Institution.

Trapunto is still used for decorating bedcovers, clothing, and wall hangings. Any firmly woven fabric can be worked; the choice will depend on the ultimate use. You will need two layers of fabric, one for the top and one for the backing, plus enough yarn or stuffing to fill the design. The amount of time involved depends on the intricacy of the design. If you are a beginner it's best to start with something simple. If you make a piece of clothing, do not use an intricate design or stuff so tightly that you make the item uncomfortable to wear.

Mary Ann Takacs attended the Fashion Institute of Technology in New York, where she majored in apparel design. She has a fine arts education degree from Montclair State College, Montclair, New Jersey. Ms. Takacs has worked for McCall's Needlework & Crafts as a designer. She also teaches sewing and designs clothing.

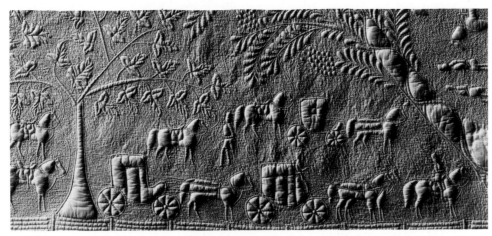

This detail is from a white cotton trapunto quilt made by Virginia Ivey in 1856. It is titled *A Representation of the Fair Ground Near Russellville, Kentucky.*

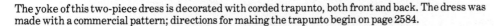

The yoke of this two-piece dress is decorated with corded trapunto, both front and back. The dress was made with a commercial pattern; directions for making the trapunto begin on page 2584.

Needlecrafts
Trapunto sheet and pillowcases

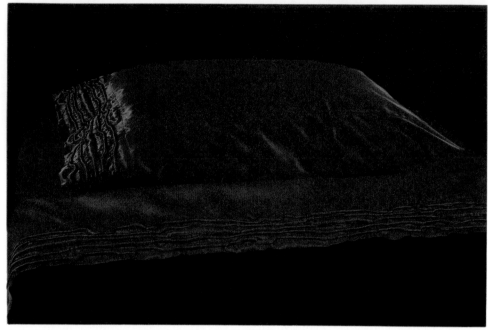

A shrimp-colored satin sheet and pillowcase are decorated with flowing lines of trapunto. This design was stitched with contrasting dark-brown thread in a heavy weight to emphasize the design. The same design could be stitched with thread matching the fabric color.

Five freely flowing lines threaded with rug yarn make the trapunto design that edges the sheet and pillowcase pictured above. The middle line widens at intervals; these areas are stuffed with loose polyester fiber. The design pictured was worked on shrimp-colored satin sheets; it could be used on any commercially made sheets and pillowcases that are a solid color. For this project, you need: one top sheet and two matching pillowcases; one yard of sheer lining fabric in a color close to that of the sheet; 60 yards (six 10-yard spools) of silk buttonhole-twist thread in a contrasting color, for the bobbin; one large spool of polyester-and-cotton thread in the same contrasting color, for threading the machine's needle; one small spool of polyester-and-cotton thread the same color as the sheet, for sewing the hems; basting thread; 120 yards of synthetic rug yarn in a color similar to that of the sheet; and loose polyester fiber for stuffing. The equipment you will need, in addition to a sewing machine, includes tracing paper and tracing wheel; ruler; pencil; a fine-point water-

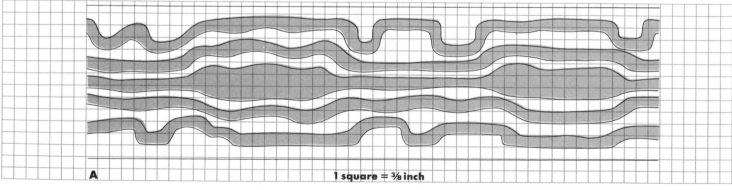

A

1 square = ⅜ inch

Figure A: To enlarge this pattern for the trapunto design on the sheet and pillowcases, make a grid of ⅜-inch squares; then copy the design, square by square, onto the larger grid. The design is repeated along the hem of the top sheet and around the hem of the pillowcases by flipping the pattern over at each repeat. The wider areas are stuffed; the lines are corded.

proof felt-tipped marker; fabric shears; pins; a sewing needle; a large-eyed rug needle; small embroidery scissors; and a stuffing tool such as a knitting needle or a letter opener.

To prepare the top sheet for the design, open the top hem and press out the fold line. Open the side seams about 12 inches down either side. Press in a new 5-inch hem, plus ½ inch to turn under at the edge. Commercial sheets have a top hem of about three inches; so this procedure will shorten the overall length by about 2 inches. Open the side seams and hems of the pillowcases, press out the fold lines; then press in new 5½-inch hems, the same as on the top sheet.

On the 1 yard piece of lining fabric, rule 5-inch-wide strips parallel with the selvage. These will be 35 inches long, plus a ½-inch seam allowance at either end. Cut out these strips and stitch them together until you have one strip long enough to back the new hem on the top sheet and two strips long enough to do the same on the opened pillowcases. Press the seams of these strips open and lay them flat on your work surface. Enlarge the pattern (Figure A) onto tracing paper; then go over the lines with a felt-tipped marker on both sides of the paper so you will still be able to see the design after you place the sheer lining strip over it. Place the sheer lining strip prepared for the sheet over the enlarged pattern. Trace the pattern onto the strip using the fine-point felt-tipped marker. When you reach the end of the pattern, flip it over so pattern lines can be matched to the ends of the design already traced. Continue tracing the pattern until the strip is covered. As Figure B shows, place the top sheet face down and lay the lining strip, design side up, on top of it, below the crease that marks the new hem allowance. Leave ½ inch of the sheet free on either end for the edge seam to come. Pin the strip in place; then baste it across its width, using a long pad stitch (Figure C). This basting will help keep the strip stationary as you sew the design. Wind the bobbin with the silk-twist thread; then thread the machine with the matching polyester-and-cotton thread. Loosen the presser-foot pressure knob to free the needle for sewing curves. Check the tension by stitching on a scrap of fabric; adjust if necessary. With the patterned strip on top of the sheet, stitch along all ten design lines. When you come to a curve, firmly hold the fabric with both hands and guide it through the machine (photograph 1). When you reach the end of a line, leave a tail of thread long enough to tie. When all ten rows are complete, pull the silk-twist thread through to the back, tie it to the stitching thread, and clip the threads close to the knot.

Cording the Design

To cord the lines of the design, thread a large-eyed needle with two long strands of rug yarn, doubled so you are working with four strands. With embroidery scissors, make ¼-inch openings about every 3 inches along all five rows. Thread the rug yarn through the first row between the sheet and the lining strip, starting at the edge and coming out at the first opening (photograph 2). Pull on each of the four strands to make sure the yarn is smooth. Then put the needle back into the same opening and bring it out at the next one.

Pull the yarn through (photograph 3). When you come to a sharp curve, use the point of the needle to ease the yarn smoothly into the curve (photograph 4, page 2584). When you run out of yarn, clip the ends close to the fabric; then use the

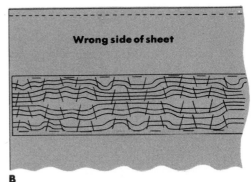

B

Figure B: Lay the marked sheer lining strip on the inside of the sheet, just below the crease ironed for the 5-inch hem. Pin and baste the strip in place, allowing ½ inch at each end for restoring the side hems.

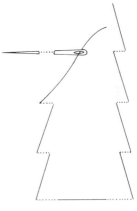

C

Figure C: The long pad stitch illustrated above is used for basting across the width of the lining strip to hold it in place.

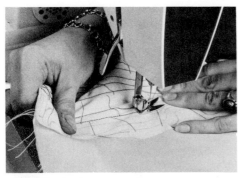

1: Hold the fabric firmly with both hands so you can guide it through the sewing machine as you follow the curves of the design lines.

2: Thread four strands of rug yarn into the first row, between the sheet and lining fabric. Come up through the first ¼-inch slit in the lining fabric.

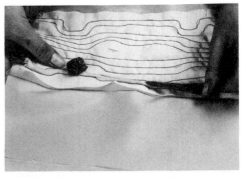

3: Take the yarn back into the first slit and up through the second slit. To smooth the yarn in the channel, pull on each strand individually.

4: To make sure the yarn follows the curves of the design and fills them, use the needle to push the yarn into the curves.

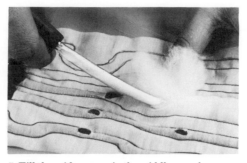

5: Fill the wider areas in the middle rows by using a tool such as a letter opener to push small amounts of polyester fiber into the pocket.

6: To keep the stuffing from coming out, close the opening with an overcasting stitch, using a regular needle and sewing thread.

needle to poke the ends between the lining and the sheet. Start new strands at that point, being careful to avoid both overlaps and gaps. To fill the center line, thread yarn through the narrow areas, using the same procedure. For the wider areas, make a ½- to ¾-inch slit in the center. Using a stuffing tool such as a knitting needle or a letter opener, poke in small amounts of loose polyester fiber until the pocket is filled (photograph 5). To keep the stuffing in place, sew the opening closed with an overcasting stitch (photograph 6). If yarn openings are small, there is no need to sew them closed. When the design is all corded and stuffed, turn the side seams in ½ inch and stitch them in place. Fold the top hem down to cover the lining. Fold under the ½-inch seam allowance, and pin the hem in place. Baste, then stitch it, using polyester-and-cotton thread the same color as the sheets.

Pillowcases
Trace the design onto the sheer lining strips for the pillowcases the same way, but adjust the lines so the right and left ends will line up when the side seam of the pillowcase is sewn. Cord and stuff the design as you did the top sheet. Resew the side seams; then fold down the hem, turn under the seam and stitch, using thread that matches the fabric.

Needlecrafts
A yoked dress

The two-piece dress shown on page 2580 and at left has a corded trapunto design worked on the yoke of both the front and back of the blouse. The dress was made with a commercial pattern. To make a trapunto blouse, shirt, or dress, buy a pattern in your size with a front and back yoke. Select the fabric and notions specified by that pattern. In addition, for the trapunto, you will need: ½ yard of sheer light-weight interfacing; ½ yard of lining fabric; and 2 ounces of 4-ply acrylic yarn in a color similar to that of the fabric.

The dress pictured is made of a polyester knit fabric with some elasticity. If you use a woven fabric, the design may look even more sculptured. Work the trapunto decoration before you assemble the dress; the cording causes a slight take-up in fabric, but you can adjust the dress to fit with smaller seams.

To begin, cut all the pattern pieces out of the dress fabric, following the pattern directions. Also cut the front and back yokes out of lightweight interfacing and sew the yokes together at the shoulder seams. Do not stitch any darts. Stitch the dress-fabric yoke pieces together the same way, and press all the seams open. Enlarge the trapunto design (Figure D). Place the design over the fabric yoke to see how it fits. If the design is too long you might want to end it with the petal cluster rather than having the vine continue down the yoke. Depending on the size of the pattern you are working with, you may have to adjust the design as it goes over the shoulder seam. You can lengthen or shorten the vine as necessary. When the design is centered on the yoke, trace it onto the interfacing, using a fine-point felt-tipped marker.

Place the fabric and interfacing yokes together, wrong sides facing, so the

Corded lines of trapunto, shown on the front of a dress on page 2580, continue over the dress shoulder and meet to form a flower shape on the back yoke.

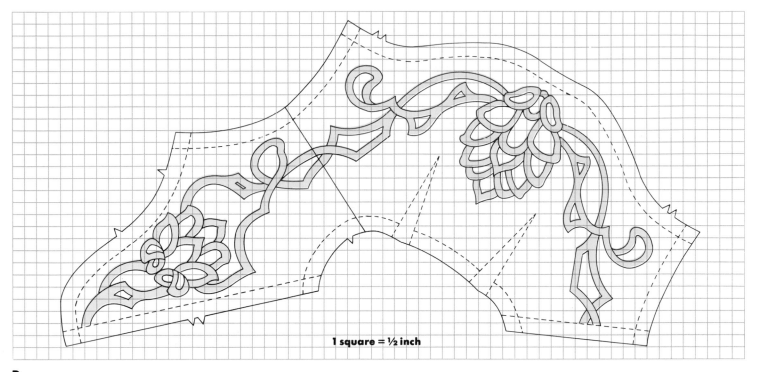

1 square = ½ inch

D

Figure D: To enlarge this design for the dress yoke, draw a grid of ½-inch squares on paper and copy the design, square by square, onto the larger grid. Place this design on your yoke-pattern piece to make sure that it can be centered on it the way it is centered on the pattern piece above.

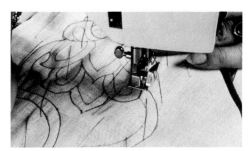

7: Stitch the design for the dress trapunto onto the fabric and interfacing, with the latter on top. To avoid an excessive number of thread ends, stitch a continuous line along the top of the petal cluster.

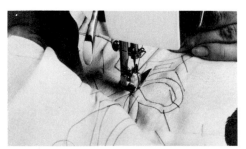

8: To end a line of stitching without knotting the thread, hold the fabric firmly in one place and make several stitches. Clip the thread off close to the fabric.

9: To cord an intricate design like this, with many turns in the design line, follow one path as far as possible; then cut off the yarn and tuck the ends inside.

design on the interfacing is on top. Pin and baste the two together, using a long pad stitch (Figure C, page 2583). Using polyester-and-cotton sewing thread in both the bobbin and the needle, stitch the design. Do not sew each petal separately; that would leave too many beginning and ending threads. Rather, try to stitch as many continuous lines as you can by pivoting the fabric when the design line changes direction (photograph 7). To end a line without knotting the thread, hold the fabric firmly and make several stitches in one place (photograph 8); then clip the thread close to the stitches.

The cording used in this design is four strands of 4-ply acrylic knitting worsted. Cut ¼-inch slits in the interfacing. Thread a large-eyed needle with two long strands of yarn, doubled over, and thread the needle through the slits in the interfacing, as pictured on page 2583. When the lines of the design fork in two directions, pull the yarn through one line (photograph 9). Then cut the yarn and thread the other portion of the line as though you were starting a new line (photograph 10).

When the cording is completed, cut the yoke pieces out of lining fabric and stitch the shoulder seams. Place the lining over the trapunto to keep it from fraying, and stitch all three layers together ¼ inch from the edge. Treat this as one layer of fabric as you continue to assemble the dress, following the commercial pattern.

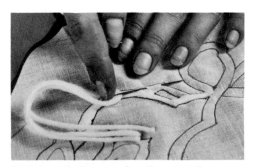

10: To cord the by-passed section, start the yarn as though you were starting a new line. From the front, the trapunto will appear to be continuous; the beginnings and endings will not show.

2585

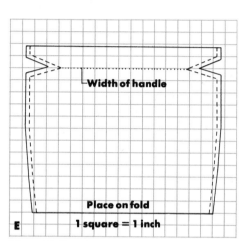

Figure E: To enlarge this pattern for the handbag shown at right, make a grid with 1-inch squares; then copy the shape, square by square, onto the larger grid.

Needlecrafts
Batik handbag

The pattern of a fabric can itself suggest a trapunto design. Above, a small piece of fabric batiked by the craftswoman was used to make a trapunto handbag, with stuffing and cording to emphasize the fabric design. Any commercial fabric can be enhanced with trapunto.

You can use trapunto with a patterned fabric by stuffing and cording in such a way that you enhance that pattern. The handbag shown above was made from a 16-by-24-inch piece of batik; the light-blue lines were corded and the purple squares stuffed. To make a similar handbag, you will need: patterned fabric 16 by 24 inches; a 16-by-24-inch piece of medium-weight interfacing; a 16-by-24-inch piece of lining fabric; sewing thread to match the outer fabric; rug yarn; loose polyester fiber; basting thread; wooden handles (available at notions departments or from mail-order needlework shops); dressmaker's carbon; and a tracing wheel.

Enlarge the pattern for the handbag (Figure E). Make sure the width across the top of the pattern between the notches is the same as that of the wooden handles. If not, adjust the pattern to fit by making it wider or narrower. Trace the pattern onto the patterned fabric, the interfacing, and the lining, and cut out each piece. With carbon paper and tracing wheel, mark the seam lines on each piece.

Pin the interfacing to the wrong side of the fabric and baste the two together with a long pad stitch (Figure C, page 2583). With the patterned fabric facing you, outline the areas to be stuffed or corded with machine stitching. The double lines that will encase cording should be ¼ inch or less apart if you are going to use two strands of rug yarn, ¼ to ⅜ inch apart if you will use four strands. In this design, the light-blue lines were corded and the purple rectangles were stuffed. Stuff or cord the design as described on page 2583; do not go beyond the seam lines or the stuffing or cording will get caught in the seam. Stitch the side seams of the trapunto fabric and the lining. Press the seams. Slip the lining inside the handbag, wrong sides facing. To attach the handles, follow the manufacturer's directions.

Needlecrafts
Lion T-shirt

A regal lion with a trapunto mane is appliquéd to a T-shirt; ruffles made of the same fabric as the lion's body are added to the sleeves.

Jermaine Sonnenschein designs pillows for individuals and interior decorators, and has exhibited at the Brooklyn Heights Promenade Art Show and the Washington Square Outdoor Art Show, both in New York. She also designs T-shirts for several boutiques in New York.

11: This closeup view of the lion appliqué shows the positioning of the fabric shapes.

Just a small amount of trapunto can be an effective design element. The pert lion shown above was appliquéd on a T-shirt; then the lion's mane was stuffed with polyester fiber to give it shape.

To decorate a T-shirt with a lion, you will need: ½ yard of cotton fabric for the lion's body and the ruffles on the sleeves; a scrap of velour fabric for the mane and the tail; a scrap of green or green-print fabric for the plants; a 12-inch square of lightweight nonwoven interfacing; fusible web; sewing thread in colors that coordinate with the fabrics; ½ yard of ½-inch-wide grosgrain ribbon; and a small amount of polyester fiber.

To start, enlarge the patterns for the lion appliqué (Figure F, page 2588). Cut each shape out of the appropriate fabric. Using photograph 11 as a guide, place the shapes on the T-shirt. If you place a small piece of fusible web under each piece and secure it with a warm iron, following package directions, the pieces will remain in place without being pinned. When the fabric shapes are secure, turn the T-shirt inside out and center the 12-inch square of nonwoven interfacing over the appliqué area. Pin the square along its outside edges, keeping the pins outside the design area. Turn the T-shirt right side out and appliqué each piece in place, using the zigzag stitch on your sewing machine or sewing by hand.

When the stitching is completed, turn the T-shirt inside out and trim the interfacing close to the stitching around the outside edge of the appliqué. Slit the

12: After you trim the interfacing close to the outermost appliqué stitching, slit the interfacing behind the lion's mane and loosely stuff it with polyester fiber.

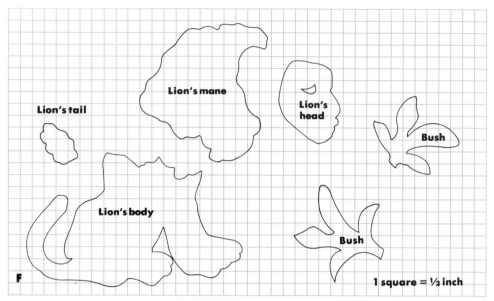

Figure F: To enlarge these patterns for the lion appliqué, draw a grid with ½-inch squares on paper and copy the shapes, square by square, onto the larger grid. Then cut out each piece, pin it to the appropriate fabric, and cut out the fabric shape.

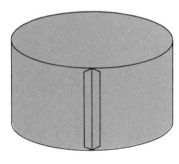

Figure G: For a ruffle, cut a 5-by-18½-inch piece of fabric and join the ends with a ½-inch seam (left). Press the seam open. Fold the ring in half lengthwise, with wrong sides facing, and press (center). Machine-stitch two rows of basting stitches, keeping both rows within ½ inch of the raw fabric edges. Pull the top thread to gather the ruffle (right).

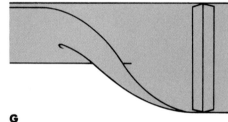

Figure H: Stitch the ruffle to the T-shirt cuff, putting the raw edge of the ruffle over the cuff and covering it with a length of grosgrain ribbon. Stitch along both edges of the ribbon.

interfacing behind the lion's mane so you can put in the polyester fiber (photograph 12). If you like, slit the interfacing on the lion's tail and stuff it with polyester fiber as well. Close the openings with an overcast stitch.

To make sleeve ruffles, cut two 5-by-18½-inch pieces of fabric. Stitch each piece together at the ends, with a ½-inch seam, to make two rings (Figure G, left). Press the seam open. Fold the ring in half lengthwise, with wrong sides facing. Using the largest stitch on your sewing machine or stitching by hand, make two rows of basting stitches on the raw edges of the fabric (Figure G, center). Knot the bottom threads together and pull the top threads, gathering the ruffle along these threads until it fits the T-shirt cuff (Figure G, right).

Cut the grosgrain ribbon in half, and use it to attach the ruffles to the sleeves (Figure H). Stitch along both edges of the ribbon, folding the raw end under where it meets the beginning of the ribbon.

Needlecrafts
Face pillow

$ ⏳ 👤 🎨

A trapunto pillow in the shape of a face is a sure conversation-starter. The 14-by-18-inch pillow shown opposite has a top layer of sheer white voile and a lining of cocoa-brown cotton. In some places the lining shows through, adding to the three-dimensional effect.

A trapunto pillow that resembles a face is one way to add personality to a unique decorating accessory.

To make a pillow similar to this one, you will need: ½ yard of voile, organdy, or other sheer, sturdy fabric; ½ yard of cotton or other medium-weight fabric in brown, black, or gray, for the lining; ½ yard of fabric for the pillow backing; a one-pound package of polyester fiber; and white sewing thread. To transfer your face drawing to the fabric, you need dressmaker's carbon paper in a light color and a tracing wheel.

Draw a pattern for the face you want to make on a large piece of paper, approximately the size you want the pillow to be. Place the lining fabric on a flat work surface with the dressmaker's carbon paper on top of it, carbon-side down. Put the drawing, right side up, on top and go over all the lines with the tracing wheel.

Place the lining, design side up, on top of the sheer fabric. Pin the two layers together securely, being careful not to put any pins on the lines of the design. Using white thread, with the lining fabric facing you, machine-stitch along all of the lines. Each time you end a thread, leave a tail about 4 inches long. When the stitching is completed, knot all of the thread tails on the back, and clip them close to the fabric. If the threads are not knotted, they will unravel, destroying the sharpness of the design.

Cut a slit in the lining fabric in each area to be filled. Stuff these areas one by one with polyester fiber, using a knitting needle to help push the stuffing in. Use stuffing to define facial areas; the nose and lips of the face pictured were stuffed tightly, but the cheeks were loosely filled. To accentuate the eyes, the irises were stuffed but the rest of the eyeballs were not. The hair was loosely filled to achieve a softer look. To keep the polyester fiber in place, stitch the slits closed with an overcast stitch (photograph 13).

To make the trapunto into a pillow, trim the fabric edge, leaving a ½-inch seam allowance. Place the trimmed trapunto, right side down, on top of the pillow backing fabric. Stitch around the trapunto, following the overall shape of the head and leaving an 8-inch opening. Trim the backing fabric; turn the pillow right side out, and stitch the opening closed by hand.

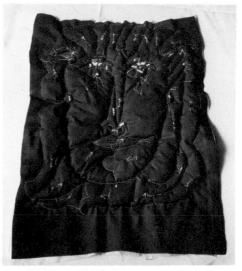

13: After the face design is stitched, slit open the backing fabric over each of the areas, stuff it with polyester fiber, and close it with hand stitching.

Barbara Barrick McKie lives in Ledyard, Connecticut. Though she studied biology, her interest in crafts has dominated her life. Barbara took up quilting in 1971, to make a quilt for the bed in her new house. Intrigued with this craft, she has been quilting ever since. She has had quilts in shows in Massachusetts, Rhode Island, and Connecticut; and her quilts have appeared in Complete Guide to Quilting *and* McCall's Contemporary Quilts.

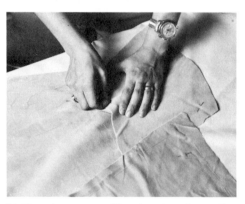

14: To make a crazy quilt, cut random shapes; then overlap their edges as you pin and baste them to the lining fabric. Baste about an inch from the raw edge.

15: Turn under about ¼ inch of the raw edge of each shape and stitch it to the backing by hand, turning under any other raw edge that you meet.

Needlecrafts
Crazy-quilt wall hanging

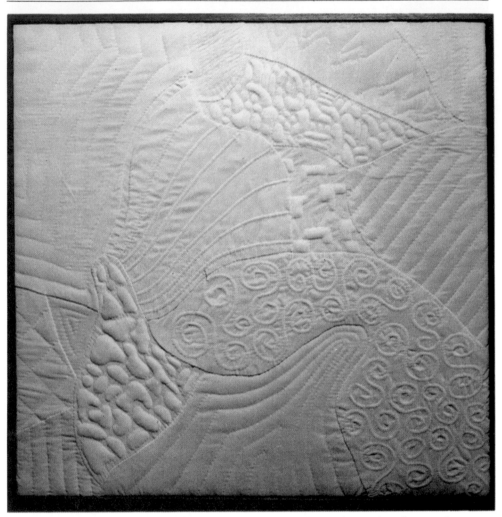

This 32-inch-square crazy-quilt wall hanging is made of white velvet cut into various shapes and sewn onto a backing fabric. Each shape has its own distinctive trapunto design.

The wall hanging shown above is a crazy-quilt design, made with random shapes cut from white velvet and stitched onto a background fabric. Then each shape was quilted with a different design and stuffed or corded according to its shape.

To make a wall hanging similar to the one above, you will need: the basic materials listed on page 2582, 1 yard of white velvet; 1 yard of backing fabric; white polyester-and-cotton sewing thread; a sewing needle and thimble; and loose polyester fiber and yarn to stuff and cord the designs. If you choose a brightly colored backing fabric, it will show through the white velvet as a muted color. So your choice of a backing fabric depends on the effect you want.

To make a crazy-quilt design, first cut the backing fabric to size—the wall hanging pictured is 32 inches square. Then cut random shapes from the top fabric. Pin these shapes to the backing fabric, overlapping all edges. Baste each shape to the backing, using long basting stitches 1 inch in from the raw edge of each shape (photograph 14). When all the pieces are basted, turn the raw edge of each piece under ¼ inch and hand-stitch it to the backing, keeping the stitches hidden in the fold as much as possible. When you cross a raw edge that has not been sewn (photograph 15), turn it under ¼ inch and continue along the edge you are working on.

To quilt the wall hanging, stitch by hand or machine a variety of patterns through both layers. Figure I shows the patterns used in this wall hanging, but yours should

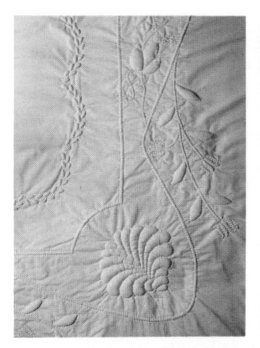

The bed quilt above combines several traditional trapunto patterns. Some of the motifs, such as the basket in the center of the quilt (above, center) were stuffed with polyester fiber. Other parts of the design along the sides and especially the corners (above, far left) were also stuffed to achieve the raised trapunto effect.

Figure I: Each shape of the white velvet wall hanging pictured was quilted with a different pattern. The small rounded shapes were stuffed with polyester fiber; the long rows were threaded with yarn.

fit the shapes of the pieces you cut, since the cording and stuffing cannot go through the stitches between pieces. Cord or stuff the channels and pockets, whichever is more appropriate for the quilting design, by slitting the backing and inserting yarn or polyester fiber (page 2583).

To finish the wall hanging, you can frame it as shown. Or you can finish the side edges with ½-inch hems, and turn the top and bottom edges under to form casings through which you can insert dowels.

For related entries, see "Appliqué" and "Quilting."

TREE HOUSES
Out on a Limb

A Victorian-era tree-house restaurant in France looks well patronized in this contemporary engraving. Such establishments, inspired by the book *Robinson Crusoe*, were frequented by fashionable Parisians and were the scene of many wedding parties.

There is something elemental and primitive about climbing up to a tree house, a secret refuge where the call of adventure can be clearly heard. Tree houses have not always been the exclusive domain of children. The nineteenth-century tree houses of Sceaux, a suburb of Paris (pictured at left), were designed as elegant perches from which restaurant patrons could view the countryside while dining on haute cuisine brought to them on dumbwaiters. And though the three tree-house projects that follow are for youngsters, their designers—all of them responsible adults—agree they felt a youthful exhilaration in building them.

Choosing the Right Kind of Structure
Appearances suggest that a tree house requires a considerable amount of enterprise to build. Yet all you need to make one is scrap lumber, a few basic household tools, and a tree. Actually, with a slight stretch of the imagination, you can build a tree house without a tree. Whole villages of stilt houses line river banks in some parts of the world, where repeated flooding would otherwise make living impossible. So if you happen not to have a massive tree, you can still build an elevated lookout on posts (page 2596) or a low platform in a clump of small trees (page 2594). For those who do have a big tree, instructions for a traditional tree house, as shown opposite, begin on page 2600.

Selecting the Site
Study the possibilities offered by each prospective tree-house site. Whether or not you have a century-old oak or stately elm, the site should be chosen for its location and the opportunity it offers for secure placement of the structure. Tree houses for younger children should be kept simple, safe, low, and in full view of the house. Older children, on the other hand, may think nothing short of total seclusion is acceptable. If you have several trees strong enough to support the weight of a tree house and several children to entertain, make your selection on the basis of the shape of the branches rather than the size of the tree. Branches that project horizontally from the main trunk are far stronger than those rising at a sharp angle from the trunk; a pair of such branches a short climb from the ground make an ideal perch. If such a combination is not available, look for any similar situation that would provide a stable support for a platform. For example, a tree house can be built supported by three or four small trees. Their location will determine the size and shape of the platform: square, rectangle, triangle, or some odd shape cut to fit the need.

Preparing the Tree
Whatever tree or trees you select, be sure they are sound. Avoid using any dead tree. Check for signs of rot by probing with a screw driver. Small areas of rot in an otherwise sound tree can be chiseled out and the good wood underneath treated with tree-wound paint (available at hardware and garden-supply stores). Most trees will require some pruning to remove interfering branches. Apply tree-wound paint to any cut surface larger than a fifty-cent piece. This will prevent moisture and insects from damaging the tree. Work only in a tree that is totally clear of overhead power lines. For convenience, when you work a distance from the ground, tie your tool box to the tree to avoid repeated trips up and down the ladder. And sling a strong rope over a branch above you so you can hoist materials tied on by a helper on the ground. Ultimately, cover the ground around the tree with a layer of peat, sawdust, or other spongy material as a safety measure.

This entrancing tree house, complete with gabled roof, was built in only a few hours from scrap materials. A rope network and wooden handrail enclose the play deck on three sides, and a lower access platform breaks the climb into two stages. Sections were built on the ground and hoisted into place. Instructions begin on page 2600.

A tree house for younger children is reassuringly close to the ground. Nestled in a cluster of young trees, it was made in an afternoon from scrap lumber.

Outdoor Activities
A tree house in a grove ¢ ☒ 👫 ✈

We wanted a tree house that would be safe, inexpensive, and within view of our kitchen window. I chose a clump of four medium-sized locust trees in our backyard and framed the tree house shown above within them. Together they formed a nearly square figure, measuring about 4 feet on a side. The deck was built 5 feet above the ground. This was high enough for the children, but low enough for me to construct without a ladder. (For older children, this kind of structure could be built higher up in a single tree, where the trunk forks into three or four strong branches.) The lumber consisted entirely of scrap pieces. For the tree house shown, built in a single afternoon, the framing required six 4-foot lengths of 2-by-4-inch lumber, the deck four 8-foot 1-by-4s, and the railing and steps three 8-foot 1-by-3s. A crosscut saw, 12- and 9-penny galvanized box nails, a chisel, a claw hammer, and a carpenter's level complete the list of tools and materials needed.

The Framing
Mark the approximate height of the platform on the inside of one tree. If necessary, use the hammer and chisel to remove a small amount of bark and wood from the tree at that point so a 2-by-4 support will fit snugly and squarely against the tree. With a single nail, temporarily attach a 2-by-4 at that point. Swing it into place against a second tree, level it with the carpenter's level, and mark the tree for necessary smoothing and the 2-by-4 for length. Remove the 2-by-4 and treat any

Charles A. Dowdall was born in Utica, New York, where he built a number of tree houses as a boy. He is a clerk with the United States Postal Service, and now lives in Sag Harbor, New York, where he continues to build tree houses and children's toys.

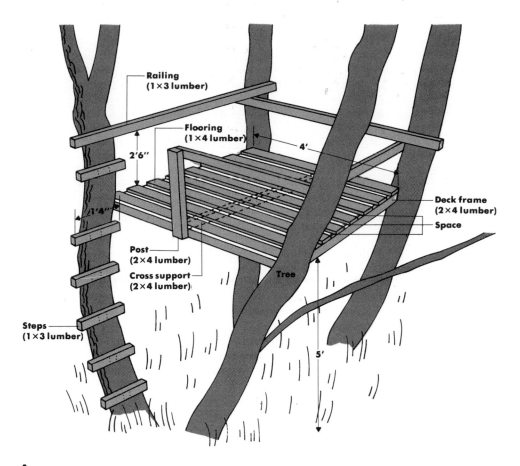

Railing
(1×3 lumber)

Flooring
(1×4 lumber)

4'

2'6"

1'4"

Deck frame
(2×4 lumber)

Space

Post
(2×4 lumber)

Cross support
(2×4 lumber)

Tree

Steps
(1×3 lumber)

5'

A
Figure A: The construction of the tree house in a grove begins by nailing the deck frame to four trees and adding the flooring of the platform, as shown. A low railing fastened to the trees (and a post on the entry side) is added, and six slat steps are secured to the trunk nearest the entrance.

exposed wood with tree-wound paint; then cut the 2-by-4 to size. When it is nailed permanently in place, it should extend slightly beyond each tree trunk. Nail it broadside to the inside of both trees with four or five 12-penny nails through each end (Figure A). For extra strength, drive the nails at a slight angle from various directions. Be sure no nail heads or points protrude.

In the same way, nail a second 2-by-4 to the opposite pair of trees. This time, in addition to checking the leveling of the board itself, make sure it is at the same height as the first board. Don't trust the ground to be level; use a third board and the level to establish the proper height of the second. The remaining two sides of the frame may be nailed to the outside of the trees, or be fitted between the ends of the first two boards, whichever works better. If you plan to anchor your platform in a clump of three trees, build a supporting triangle of three 2-by-4s.

For a deck measuring 6-by-6 feet or less, one extra cross support is adequate. Cut this piece to size so it spans the sides of the frame (the last two members) and is parallel to and midway between the ends (the first two members). For larger decks, use additional cross supports, spaced evenly between the end members.

The Deck and Railing
For the deck, cut the 1-by-4 boards to length so they span the frame end to end, and nail the boards to the 2-by-4s. Leave a 1-inch space between the boards for drainage, drive four 8-penny nails through each end of the deck boards into the 2-by-4s, and use additional nails to anchor the edge boards to the side 2-by-4s. Angle the nails as before.

If your trees are relatively straight, you can use them as posts for mounting the guard railing. Attach the railing to the inside of the trunks so it can take maximum outward stress. Cut 1-by-3s to span the spaces between the trees on three sides of the platform. Position them 2½ feet above the platform, check for level, and nail them broadside to the trees, using four or five 12-penny nails driven from various angles. The fourth side remains partly open to permit access to the platform. To make a railing partway across this opening, as I did, you need a vertical post. Cut a 2-foot 9½-inch length of 2-by-4 and nail it to the outside of the frame with four or five 12-penny nails. A good place for this joint is the point where the middle cross support meets the frame member. Then cut the last piece of railing to span the opening between post and tree, and fasten it in place with four or five 12-penny nails.

(If the trees angle sharply away from the deck, erect 2-by-4 posts at each corner of the deck, using the method described above.)

If small children might be using the tree house, you can make it even safer by stapling chicken wire around the outside between the railing and the deck, leaving open only the access space. Cut the wire to size with a tin snips. Bend over any sharp ends with pliers.

The Steps

For access, an old wooden ladder, cut to the proper length, can be nailed to the frame, or a rope ladder can be suspended from the deck. Simpler still are the steps I used: six 16-inch lengths of 1-by-3 lumber nailed at intervals to the tree trunk adjacent to the entrance. Center each step on the trunk (flattening the trunk a bit if necessary), and fasten it securely with four or five 12-penny nails, spaced as far across the trunk as possible for rigidity.

Sand away any splinters on the tree house. You may decide to paint the steps, platform, and railing with two coats of exterior paint, in a combination of bright colors. I left our tree house unpainted to make it as unobtrusive as possible.

Outdoor Activities
A platform roost $ ● ♟ ✈

Not every bird lives in a tree. Aeries, roosts, and nests can be found on windswept mountain tops, hidden in thickets, and tucked under eaves. Since our weekend house is in the scrubby pine barrens of a coastal area, there were no suitable trees nearby for a tree house. So we constructed a platform atop 16-foot cedar posts set in concrete, as shown opposite.

All the lumber was standard 8-foot or 16-foot lengths. This meant a minimum of cutting in working with the basically square design. To make a platform roost like ours you will need: six 16-foot lengths of 4-by-4-inch cedar; twelve 8-foot lengths of 2-by-4-inch lumber; six 4-by-8 sheets of exterior-grade plywood, four of them ½ inch thick and two ⅝ inch thick; four 8-by-8-by-16-inch cinder blocks; two 40-pound bags of ready-mix concrete; four 8-inch bolts with matching nuts and washers; 10- and 16-penny galvanized box nails; a 12-foot stepladder and, in addition to the tools listed in the previous project, a post-hole digger, a power drill and bit to match the diameter of the bolts, and a coping saw or keyhole saw. The lumber should be treated in advance with creosote wood preservative available at lumber yards, to forestall rot.

Erecting the Posts

On a level site, mark a 7-foot 9½-inch square. Use a post-hole digger to make holes centered on the four corners. Dig the holes 4 feet deep and 18 by 10 inches across, large enough so you can place an 8-by-8-by-16-inch cinder block at the bottom (Figure B). Be sure the bottoms of the holes are reasonably level so the blocks can rest solidly. Set a cinder block in each posthole, with the holes in the block facing sideways. Tamp the blocks with the end of a board as necessary to set them, and check them with a level. Mix the concrete, half a bag at a time, following the manufacturer's directions on the bag. A metal wheelbarrow makes a good mixing trough. When the concrete is the consistency of a thick batter, place a cedar post in the center of a hole so its end rests on a cinder block. Prop the post from three sides, using 8-foot 2-by-4s to hold it erect temporarily. Check for a true vertical with a level on two adjacent sides; adjust the post (and supports) until it stands perfectly straight. Gently pour the concrete into the hole. The quantity mixed will cover the concrete block and about 1 foot of the post. Check the post again with a level before the concrete hardens; slight adjustments are still possible. Erect the three other

Tom Carr is a New York detective and a part-time student at Hunter College, where he is training for a second career in nursing. An avid sportsman, he has won several swimming and handball awards and is involved with many Cub Scout projects.

corner posts in the same way. As you set them, be sure the distance between posts does not exceed 7 feet 5 inches. Allow the concrete to harden for 24 to 48 hours before continuing construction. A fine misting with a garden hose from time to time will help the concrete cure properly. After 24 hours, you can fill the hole with soil around the post, tamping it firmly and moistening it well.

The Framing

You will have to decide which way you want the roost to face. We placed the entrance side in view of the house. Assuming you will do the same, I will call the entrance side the front and the opposite side, with its long crossbeam from which the swing and trapeze hang, the back.

Begin construction at the back, using a stepladder. On the front face of one of the back corner posts, measure up 8 feet and mark it with a pencil. At this point drill a centered hole from front to back, using a bit with the same diameter as the bolts. Select one of the two remaining 16-foot cedar posts as your back crossbeam. Mark this crossbeam 4 feet 1¾ inches from one end, and drill a centered hole at this point. Place the beam on the ground along the front faces of the back posts, with the drilled hole about 2 feet outside the drilled post. Carefully lift the drilled end of the horizontal beam up the ladder, and bolt it to the post. Leave the nut loose so the beam can be moved. Then stand the ladder beside the other back post and lift the free end of the beam to a height of about 8 feet, pivoting it on the bolted end. Lay a carpenter's level on the beam and adjust the height of the free end. When it is horizontal, mark the crossing point on both members. Lower the crossbeam's free end to the ground. Measure and drill matching holes through the two marked members as before. Raise the beam into position and bolt it tightly to the second post; then tighten the bolt on the first post. Figure C (page 2598) shows a top view of how the beam meets the posts.

Cut the remaining 16-foot cedar beam in half and, following the above method, bolt the end of one 8-foot length at the same height to the back faces of the two front posts (Figure C). To make sure the two beams are at the same height, hold a 2-by-4 even with the back beam, level it, and mark a front post. The front beam does not extend past the posts like the back one does.

If you lack a suitable perch for a tree house, a platform on stilts will give you an equivalent lift. These photographs show such a structure, the *Shark's Nest*, which is simply an enclosed deck supported by four concrete-anchored posts.

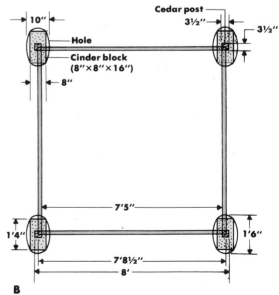

B
Figure B: Begin construction of the platform roost by marking off a 7-foot 8½-inch square on level ground. Dig holes 4 feet deep, centered at each corner. Make the holes about 10 inches wide and 18 inches long, as shown, so a cinder block can be placed at the bottom of each. Set the posts in a concrete foundation at the center of each hole so the inner dimension of the square they enclose is 7 feet 5 inches and the outer dimension 8 feet.

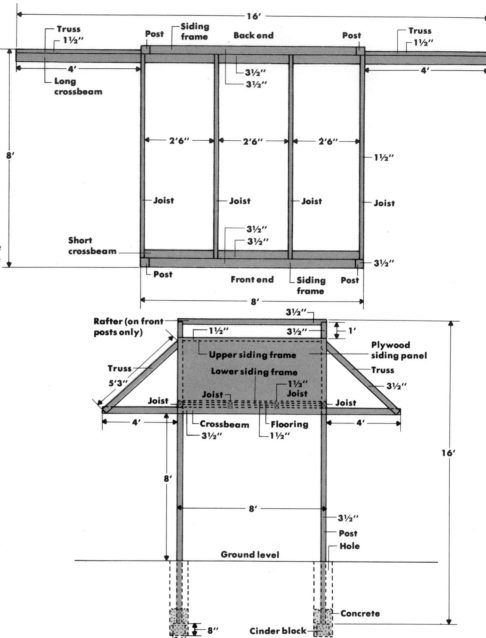

C
Figure C: The aerial view of the platform framing shows the relationship of key parts. At a height of 8 feet, bolt a 16-foot crossbeam across the two back posts, with equal overhang on either side, and an 8-foot beam to the two front posts. Nail four floor joists on and across the beams. After the flooring is nailed down, fasten siding frames to the two back posts and the two front posts, and trusses from both ends of the rear beam to each of the back posts.

D
Figure D: A rear view of the platform roost shows the posts rising from their cinder block base and tied together by crossbeams and floor joists at the 8-foot level. Also shown are the location of trusses, flooring, siding frames, siding panels, and a rafter which spans the front posts only.

To add the angled braces for the back beam (Figure D) cut two lengths of 2-by-4 lumber long enough to reach from the end of the beam to a point of the adjacent post about 1 foot from the top. These braces will be about 5 feet 3 inches long. Mark and cut the top end of each brace so it fits flush against the side of the post. Beveling is not necessary on the bottom end, for it will be nailed to the outside face of the beam. (The broad sides of the braces should face sideways, not up and down.) Attach the braces to the beams and posts with four or five 16-penny nails at each joint. Next, cut four lengths of 2-by-4 lumber to bridge the two beams and rest on top of them, the ends flush with their outer faces. These will each measure about 7 feet 5 inches, but it is better to try them on for fit before cutting. They will serve as floor joists for the platform. When all four are cut, lay them on top of the beams with their narrow sides facing up. (These pieces are marked with a ⊠ symbol in Figure D). Position the two outermost joists flush with the outside faces of the four posts, and space the inner joists between them 2½ feet apart. Fasten these joists to the beams, and where possible to the posts, with four or five 16-penny nails at each point. Drive the nails at various angles for greater rigidity.

The Platform

The platform will consist of two 4-by-8-foot sheets of ⅝-inch plywood nailed side by side across the tops of the joists. But before lifting each sheet into place, cut away 3½-inch squares at two corners. This is to fit around the corner posts. Then lift the plywood, notched corners to the outside, atop the joists, and nail both sheets into place. Drive 10-penny nails at 6-inch intervals through the plywood and into the center of each joist. Nail the full length of all four joists. If you find the middle joists hard to hit with the nails, mark guidelines across the plywood sheets 2 feet 8¼ inches in from the side edges of the platform.

Siding

The siding, which will also consist of plywood sheets, is already partly framed. To complete the frame, attach 2-by-4s, broad side up, to the front and back sides of the roost, between the posts and directly under the protruding edge of the platform. These will need to be about 7 feet 5 inches long, but cut them to fit the space between the posts. Fasten them first to each post with four or five 16-penny nails driven at various angles; then angle two nails from below into the end of each inner floor joist to keep the support board from sagging.

Next, mark lines on the outer faces of all four posts at a height of 4 feet above the bottom edge of the crossbeams. Attach 2-by-4 railings, narrow side up, to all four sides of the roost so that their top edges are flush with the marked lines and their outer edges even with those of the posts. Again, to make secure joints, angle in four or five 16-penny nails per joint.

The siding is attached much in the same way as the flooring. The back panel needs no special preparation. While standing on the deck, nail it to the outside of the frame, first along the top edge, which will come flush with the top edge of the upper railing. Then, working from a ladder on the outside, nail the sides and bottom of the panel to the posts and lower supports. Again, drive 10-penny nails at 6-inch intervals. The side panels require some advance cutting so they fit over both the long crossbeam and the trusses. Hold each panel in place at the proper height alongside the truss, and mark the locations where cutouts are necessary. Make the cuts, return the panels to their places, and nail them as before. The front panel needs the most work. Since it will have to be shortened or cut in two to provide a door opening, it presents a good opportunity to introduce a special detail at the same time, such as the swinging panel pictured on page 2597. (If you have scrap plywood around the house, perhaps the top of an old game table, you may not even need to buy a plywood sheet for this side; the dimensions given are quite arbitrary.) To make the arrangement shown, cut the plywood sheet crosswise into a 1-by-4-foot strip and a 3-by-4-foot strip, and attach these vertically to the outsides of the front framing, leaving about a 4-foot opening between them. For a trap door that swings inward only, as part of the entrance way, hang a 2 by 3½-foot strip of plywood vertically from the upper railing; this will leave a 2-foot door opening to one side of it. Use 6-inch leather or canvas strips and staples or nails for fastenings, and nail a 2-by-4 stop to the edge of the deck to hold the door inside the railing and to prevent it from swinging dangerously beyond the edge of the platform. Cap the front side of the roost with a rafter (the remaining length of 4-by-4), both for structural strength and for use as a ladder support. At each end of the rafter, cut away the last 3½ inches to a depth of 1¾ inches to fit over the top of the posts and to help form a strong joint with them. This can be done easily with two saw cuts. Secure the rafter with 16-penny nails as before.

A rope ladder for access to the roost, two types of swings, and a trapeze, can all be suspended from the various 4-by-4 crosspieces in the structure. Eyebolts, hooks, and heavy duty rope can be used, though chain link, steel cable, and cable clamps may also come in handy. Use what you have at hand or can easily obtain, but check the strength of all lines or hardware before installing them. These parts especially must be able to withstand the roughest treatment.

Have the children trace portholes with paper plates; then cut out the holes with a coping or keyhole saw (using a drill and bit to start the cut). We cut enough holes on all sides of the roost for my two children and all their friends to have individual portholes, each with a name on the outside. Portholes have a secondary function; they reduce wind resistance. The rest of the decorations were done by the children.

1: This is the well-branched tree selected for the two-level tree house shown in color on page 2593. The lowest limb on the right side was chosen as the main perch for its strength and the relatively sparse foliage above it. (Subsequent photographs were taken from the opposite side of the tree.)

2: The underside of the tree-house platform, pre-assembled on the ground, shows its sturdy construction. A square frame with two additional cross supports securely anchors the floor planks.

Outdoor Activities
A traditional tree house

As the owner-manager of an auto-body repair shop and several gas stations, Fred Krupowicz of Patchogue, New York, expresses his interest in recycling with unusual projects. Among them have been a communications center for his business, a cantilevered deck for a beach house, and the tree house pictured on page 2593.

A mature and well-branched tree offers endless possibilities for a tree house. The best location is one that affords easy access from the ground and requires a minimum of limb removal. The size and shape of the house will depend on the tree space available. It should fit snugly and securely on the supporting limbs without appearing to overwhelm the tree.

The tree I chose was the ancient beech shown in photograph 1. In it I saw the possibility of placing not only a tree house but also a lower access platform just above the first spreading of the branches. A tree house built in stages, I reasoned, would offer a broader range of play situations and greater safety. By climbing the tree and measuring, I decided that each platform could be about 4 feet square.

Tools and Materials
The tools used were the same as those listed in the previous project (page 2596). The materials, consisting entirely of scrap lumber, amounted to about 80 square feet of 2- and 1-inch-thick boards and two discarded doors. To minimize work on a ladder—always an inconvenience—I decided to do the major assembly work on the ground, hoisting finished sections into place with the help of the tree's branches and a rope. This method also permitted me to do all the painting on the ground.

Platforms
The instructions that follow are for the tree house I built, but no two trees—or scrap-lumber piles—are alike, so you will have to adapt them to fit your own situation. The construction of my two platforms was not identical, though it might have been. To make the 4-by-4-foot platform shown in photograph 2, build a frame of 2-by-4 lumber. With 10-penny nails, fasten two side pieces 4 feet long to the ends of four evenly spaced crosspieces 3 feet 9 inches long. Then nail floor boards, in this case 1-by-8-inch lumber, across the tops of the crosspieces. Cut the floor boards long enough to extend an inch or two beyond the frame. Stain or paint the platforms, as well as the other sections you build, while they are still on the ground. Then hoist each section into place (photograph 3). When you set it down on the branches, you will probably find that it is neither level nor stable. To remedy this, nail supports consisting of 2-by-4-inch or heavier lumber to individual branches and between pairs of branches to provide a secure foundation for the platform to rest on. Use a level to check these supports. To be safe, the platform should be securely nailed to strong tree limbs or intermediate supports at no fewer than four points or along three sides.

Raising the Roof
To prepare to build the roof, erect four 6-foot posts at the corners of the platform, paired on the sides rather than on the front or back (photograph 4). Check each post with a level to make sure that it is vertical; then nail it securely in place. Span each pair of posts with a crosspiece 6 inches below the top. I used 1-by-6-inch lumber for both posts and crosspieces, and nailed the wide faces of the latter to the narrow edges of the former with 10-penny nails.

A gabled roof can be made from a pair of old solid-core doors. You will have to cut them to size so there will be only a small overlap on all four sides of the tree house.

3: The platform is hoisted into the tree with the help of a rope and a strong overhanging limb. Work from a ladder while securing the platform.

4: Four 6-foot posts are nailed to the corners of the platform at the ends of two opposing sides. Cross-beams will span the other sides.

5: The preassembled gabled roof is lowered onto the posts and beams, its ridge running parallel to the beams. It will be nailed in place along both eaves and to the posts.

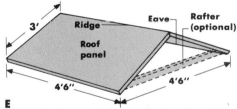

E

Figure E: The overlapping gabled roof for a 4-by-4-foot platform tree house consists of two discarded doors, each cut down to a 4½-by-3-foot size. Joining edges were beveled to fit, at around a 20-degree angle, and were nailed to each other along the ridge while the eaves were held 4 feet 6 inches apart. Rafters (dashed lines) can be added to maintain the desired eave span during nailing.

To accomplish this, I cut both doors down to 4½ feet long and 3 feet wide (Figure E). I then planed one long edge of each door to a 20-degree angle so the two would meet neatly at the peak. Then I nailed them together while a helper maintained a 4½-foot span between the bottoms of the eaves. (If you are working alone, nail a pair of rafters across the gable ends to maintain the proper eave span while you nail along the peak. Hoist the roof into place atop the four posts, and mark the angle it makes with the top of each post. Using the rope hoist again, raise the roof temporarily, and cut the posts to fit flush against the eaves. Then nail the roof to both crosspieces and to all four posts, driving 10-penny nails in pairs at 6-inch intervals (photograph 5).

Safety Barriers

Add a safety railing by nailing 4-foot lengths of 1-by-6-inch lumber between the posts on all but the entrance side. (Or you can enclose the tree house with plywood siding as in the previous project.) If you use only the handrail, you may want to weave a rope network between the railing and the deck to provide a safety barrier, while leaving the tree house open to the breeze on all sides. To do this, drill holes at fixed intervals on the railing and on the overhanging edges of the deck boards, and thread a rope consecutively through the holes as you would lace a shoe.

The ladders I used were of two types. The one that goes from the lower platform to the tree house proper consists of a pair of 2-by-4 runners, angled on both ends to meet the side of the upper platform and the top of the lower one, and spanned at 10-inch intervals with 1-by-4 treads. I fastened the treads to the runners with 10-penny nails and the runners to the platforms with 16-penny nails. The ladder that goes from the ground to the first platform is salvaged from an old work ladder. I did not nail it in place because I wanted it to be removable to prevent children from using the tree house without supervision.

Accessories can be added according to imagination and whim. Picnic baskets can easily be hoisted to the tree house, Parisian style, via a convenient limb and a length of rope.

For related projects and crafts, see the entries "Models and Mock-ups," "Plastic Pipe Constructions," "Rope Knotting," "Shelters and Tents," "Swings," and "Yard Environments."

Yet another tree-house variation is this fully enclosed tree fort. It has a sloping roof, a hinged door, and an entry porch.

TREEN WARE
Wood Workers

R. J. DeCristoforo, a master craftsman, is the author of many books and articles on crafts and home-improvement techniques. He is a consulting editor to Popular Science *magazine.*

Treen are small household objects handmade from wood, usually cooking, serving, and other household utensils. The word treen is derived from an old English word, *treow*, meaning tree or wood.

As early as 4000 B. C., shaped wooden bowls, spoons, and ladles were replacing seashells and nutshells for holding food. From that time to the seventeenth century, people who could not afford metal implements used treen. Even today, wood utensils are favored in many gourmet kitchens. Wood conducts little heat and does not add flavors to food.

Wood can be formed with hand tools to any size and contour—a fork, spoon, ladle, mixing bowl, chopping board, serving dish, or spurtle (the Scotch name for uniquely shaped mixing or stirring tools). A cook with a unique idea of the best shape or heft for a tool to mix batters, stir soups, or perform other kitchen chores can design his own treen.

Treen were originally designed for utility, but the craftsmen who made them could not resist decorating their work. A common pastime—particularly among the Welsh and Scandinavians—was to carve a wooden spoon and send it as a love token to a girl being courted. As reported by Edward H. Pinto in *Treen, or Small Woodware Throughout the Ages*, carved heart motifs signified love; wheels or spades—that the lover would work for his beloved; keys, keyholes, or tiny houses—that his home was hers; and two spoons with a single handle—that the two were one. The word spooning, which came to mean a more ardent form of courtship, is derived from the custom of carving love spoons.

The Woods Used

Treen carvers worked with the woods most readily available. In Britain, many early treen were made from oak, boxwood, beech, or sycamore. Scandinavian treen were more likely to be made of pine, birch, or alder. Countries without forests made do with driftwood. Today, you can use almost any wood. Most of the treen shown here are made of pine. This wood is easy to work and reasonably durable, although it will dent if handled carelessly. Poplar is also good. Straight-grained fir is tough and durable but a bit splintery. Maple and birch have good strength. Mahogany, teak, and walnut are often used; many imported pieces are made from them.

If you do woodworking, your scrap bin may have pieces of wood suitable for treen. I avoid open-grained woods like mahogany, oak, and walnut unless I plan to fill and seal the wood then finish it with protective coats of lacquer. Unfinished open-grained wood can be contaminated with food particles. Close-grained woods, such as pine, maple, and boxwood, can be left unfinished or given a coating of cooking oil (page 2607).

The Tools Needed

Treen can be made entirely with hand tools, although you may want to do the basic shaping with a band saw, jigsaw, or saber saw, and an electric drill. The hand tools you will need include: a crosscut saw; a coping saw with a ⅛-inch blade and about 15 teeth per inch; a brace for drilling holes with bits the sizes specified with each project; half-round wood rasp; small carving gouge; wood chisel; pocketknife; compass; vise or clamps; white glue; and a propane torch or candle if you want a burnt finish (page 2613). Much of the shaping of treen is done with sandpaper, and you will need a lot of it, in coarse (30- to 40-grit), medium (50- to 80-grit), and fine (100- to 200-grit) grades. I recommend aluminum-oxide or garnet paper with a durable cloth backing. The projects that follow may be left plain, as pictured, or you can decorate them with carved or painted designs.

These handmade kitchen utensils are characteristic of the small household objects made of wood that are called treen. From the left, the utensils are: a deep ladle, a salad fork, a stirrer, and, above the stirrer, a wide-bladed spatula.

1: Clamp the wood in a vise. Saw around the outline of the utensil as seen from the top (the deep ladle in this case) using a coping saw. Then trace the side view of the utensil on the wood and saw that out.

2: Drill terminal holes to make it easier to saw out the waste between the fork tines and in the slots that form the hook of each handle. The handle slot is filled with scrap wood to keep it from breaking when the vise is tightened.

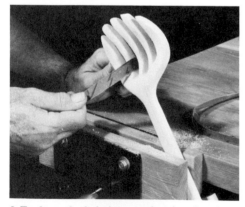

3: To shape the fork tines, work strips of sandpaper back and forth like a shoeshine rag. Sand with successively finer paper grits until the wood's surface is velvety to the touch.

While the cook stirs a heavy mix of whole-wheat dough with the spatula, a stirrer, ladle, and fork hang from a rack made for all four utensils. Their hooked handles slide into grooves cut in the front bar.

Carving and Molding
Treen for the cook

The techniques used to make the kitchen utensils shown above and in Figure A apply as well to most of the treen projects that follow. Start by cutting a block of wood to the dimensions specified, making sure the grain of the wood runs the length of the block. Each utensil pictured is cut from a 1½-by-4-by-14-inch block. For each, enlarge the pattern on the grid in Figure A. Since each utensil is symmetrical, you can if you wish, enlarge only half the pattern, cut out the half-shape and trace it on the wood. Then flip the pattern to the other side of the center line and trace it again.

Clamp the block in a vise and saw out the rough outline with a coping saw (photograph 1). Trace the enlarged side-view pattern (Figure A) on both sides of the block and saw it out. Drill any terminal holes indicated before sawing out that part and before doing any rasping or sanding. Drilling may cause splintering that can be smoothed out with rasp or sandpaper. Terminal holes drilled at the base of each fork tine and in the crook of each tool handle will help you remove the waste from these areas. Also, drill the functional holes indicated in the stirrer. If these implements may get rough handling, you can strengthen the handle crooks by drilling holes and inserting the ¼-inch reinforcing dowels as indicated.

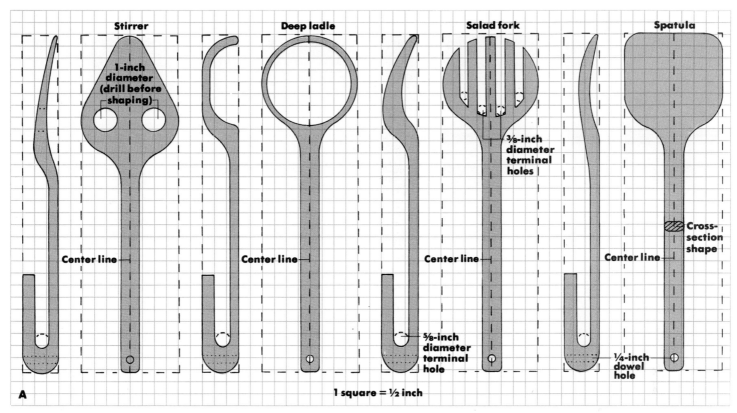

Stirrer

1-inch diameter (drill before shaping)

Center line

Deep ladle

Center line

Salad fork

⅜-inch diameter terminal holes

Center line

⅝-inch diameter terminal hole

Spatula

Cross-section shape

Center line

¼-inch dowel hole

A   1 square = ½ inch

Figure A: Each utensil, shown in top view and in side view, is cut from a 1½-by-4-by-14-inch block of wood. All handles are shaped to the same contours. To enlarge each design, draw a grid of ½-inch squares; then copy the design on the larger grid, square by square.

When you use the coping saw to remove waste between the fork tines (photograph 2) or to form the hooked handles, don't force the cuts. Too much pressure will clog the saw teeth and may break the blade.

After sawing, begin shaping the utensil with the half-round wood rasp. Work with the flat side of the rasp on flat surfaces and convex curves; use the half-round side for S curves and concave shapes. A rasp cuts only on the forward stroke; lift it on the return stroke. Apply only a little pressure; a rasp removes wood quickly. On fragile areas like the fork tines and the hooked handles, you should do most of the shaping with sandpaper (photograph 3). But use the rasp lightly to blunt all sharp corners (photograph 6, page 2608); this will speed the job of rounding them with sandpaper.

With sandpaper, smooth the rough surface left by the rasp. If you are working with hardwood, start the final smoothing with coarse paper; if it is softwood, start with medium. In either case, sand with successively finer papers (up to 150- or 200-grit), and wipe with a damp cloth after each sanding. Sand until the piece feels velvety. Exposed end-grain areas will need the most sanding.

On inside corners, edges, and curves, work with sandpaper cut into strips 1 inch, ½ inch, and ¼ inch wide. Use these strips as you would a shoeshine rag (photograph 3). This technique blends contours, giving the piece a sculptured look.

Hollowing Out the Ladle
To shape the bowl of the deep ladle, hollow it out with a curved gouge (photograph 4). Using a sharp knife, incise the wood around the edge of the area to be removed. Then holding the gouge almost vertically, press its tip into the wood alongside the knife cut to a depth of 1/16 to 1/8 inch. Bring the handle of the gouge down and its blade up as you push it forward to remove a small chip of wood. Don't try to gouge out big chunks. After working around the edge of the hollow (photograph 4), gouge from the edge toward the center from all sides so your cuts meet in the middle of the hollow. Do the final shaping and smoothing with sandpaper wrapped around your finger or the end of a rounded dowel.

4: Hollow out the bowl of the ladle with a curved carving gouge. First incise around the edge circle with a knife blade. Press the tip of the gouge into the wood to a depth of 1/16 to ⅛ inch; then bring the gouge handle down and its blade up as you push forward to remove a small chip. Work around the knife-cut edge first; then carve from the edge to the center.

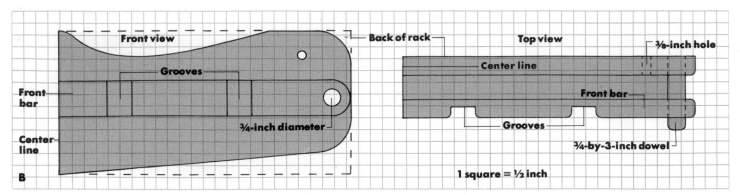

Figure B: A front view and top view of half of the rack are shown above. The two pieces are held together with a dowel at each end. To enlarge the pattern for the back piece, draw a grid of ½-inch squares; then copy the design onto the larger grid one square at a time. Cut out the half shape, trace it on the wood block, then flip the pattern to the other side of the center line and trace the matching half.

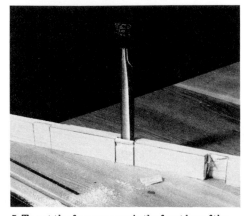

5: To cut the four grooves in the front bar of the rack, saw down ½ inch at each edge of each groove. Then remove the material between the saw cuts with a chisel. Each groove is 1 inch wide.

Rack for Kitchen Utensils

The back of the rack that holds the utensils, shown on page 2604, is cut from a ¾-by-6-by-24½-inch block of wood, its front bar from a ¾-by-1½-by-24½-inch block (Figure B). Two ¾-by-3-inch dowels join the front bar to the back at either end. Saw out the blocks of wood and drill matching ¾-inch holes for the pegs in both pieces. Then drill the ⅜-inch holes in the back that will be used for mounting the rack. Enlarge the pattern for the back piece, including the center line (Figure B). Cut out the pattern and trace it on one end of the wood block; then flip the pattern over and trace the other end. Saw out the back of the rack with a coping saw. Mark the locations of the grooves to be cut in the front bar of the rack (Figure B). Make ½-inch-deep saw cuts at each edge of each groove, and remove the waste with a chisel (photograph 5).

Sand the cutouts smooth. Saw two 3-inch lengths of ¾-inch dowel and round one end of each with sandpaper. Glue the unsanded ends in the holes in the back of the rack using white glue. Fit the front bar onto the dowels, gluing it in place. Wipe off excess glue.

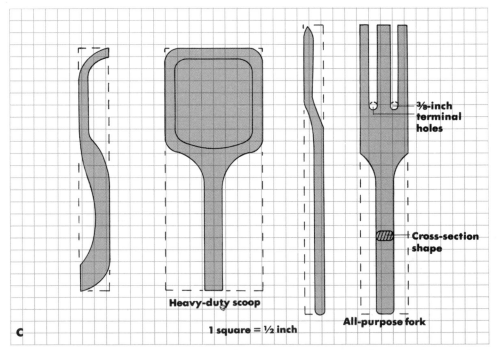

Figure C: To enlarge the pattern for the fork or the scoop, draw a grid of ½-inch squares; then copy the design onto the larger grid, one square at a time. Cut out the pattern and trace it on the wood block. Saw around the outlines shown in the top view. Then draw the side view and saw out all but the bowl of the scoop, to be hollowed with a curved gouge.

An all-purpose wooden fork and heavy-duty scoop rest in the bowl in the foreground, with a portable chopping board to the right. Hanging on the wall are five spurtles, oddly shaped mixing and stirring tools. The fork, scoop, and chopping board are unfinished; the spurtles have a cooking-oil finish.

The rack and utensils may be left unfinished or coated with cooking oil. If you oil them, rub the oil in with your hands. Then wipe away any excess with a clean, soft, lint-free cloth. Repeat the oiling once a day for a week, once a week for a month, once a month for a year, and once a year thereafter.

Fork and Scoop

Two useful pieces of treen that may be tucked in a kitchen drawer are the heavy-duty fork and scoop shown above. The tapered tip of the fork makes it useful for lifting foods as well as for mixing salads. The scoop is strong enough to be used for stirring thick mixtures vigorously. Dimensions and patterns for both utensils are given in Figure C. Following the procedures previously described, cut blocks of wood; then enlarge and trace the top-view patterns on the blocks. Drill terminal holes at the base of the fork tines. Saw out each piece with a coping saw. Enlarge, cut out, and trace the side-view patterns for each utensil. Saw out all contours except the bowl of the scoop; hollow the bowl with a gouge (page 2605). Rasp and sand each utensil to its final contours, rounding out all edges except the tips of the fork tines.

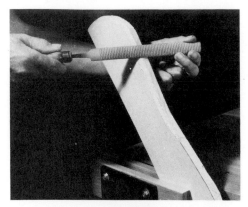

6: Use a wood rasp to round all the sharp corners on the front of the spurtle rack. Do the final shaping and smoothing with sandpaper.

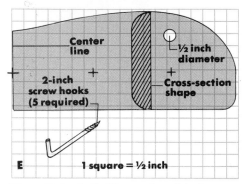

Figure E: One half of the spurtle rack is shown; enlarge it by drawing a grid of ½-inch squares, then copying the design onto the larger grid, one square at a time. Cut out the pattern; trace it on the wood. Then flip the pattern to the opposite side of the center line and trace the matching half. The cross section shows how the front of the rack is rounded with a rasp.

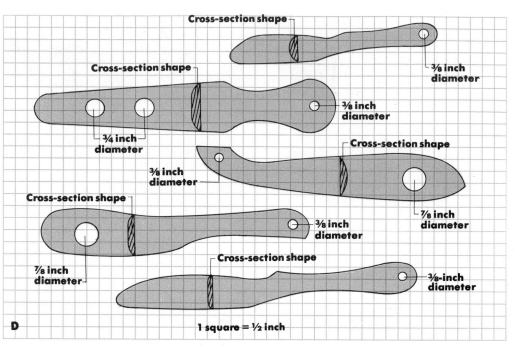

Figure D: Cut the two spurtles at the top from ⅜-inch-thick wood, the other three from ¼-inch wood. Enlarge the design for each by drawing a grid of ½-inch squares, then copying the design onto the larger grid, one square at a time. Cut out the pattern, trace it on the wood, and saw around the outlines. As the cross sections show, only one side of a spurtle is shaped with rasp and sandpaper.

Five Spurtles

Spurtles, like those hanging on the rack pictured on page 2607, can be any size or shape the cook desires; so don't hesitate to design your own.

The spurtles and their rack are detailed in Figures D and E. Follow the procedures previously described for sawing out the wood blocks, tracing the enlarged designs on them, drilling the holes, and sawing out the utensils. Spurtles vary in thickness and they are flat on one side, so no side views are shown. Instead, the curvature of each spurtle is shown as a cross-section view in Figure D. It is achieved by rasping and sanding. To make the display rack, follow the procedures given for the utensil rack on page 2606 but omit the front bar. Rasp off the outer corners (photograph 6), using the flat side of a half-round rasp, then sand. After the rack and the implements have been sanded to a velvety smoothness, insert screw hooks in the rack (Figure E) so you can hang the spurtles.

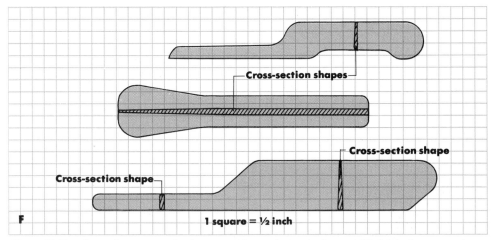

Figure F: To enlarge the patterns for these spreaders and cutters, draw a grid of ½-inch squares; then copy the design onto the larger grid, one square at a time. Cut out the pattern, trace it on the wood, and saw out the piece. Each utensil can be made from wood of the maximum thickness, shown in the enlarged cross-section views, which is then tapered with rasp and sandpaper.

These spreaders and cutters have been shaped to match what one cook felt were handy contours for various kitchen tasks.

Spreaders and Cutters

Some useful spreaders and cutters are shown above and in Figure F. To make them, follow the instructions given for the spurtles. You can vary the shapes to suit any ideas you may have about what will work best. Spreaders and cutters should be no thicker than ¼ inch at the widest part, tapering down to 1/16 inch at the narrowest. Don't try to make a knife edge on a wooden tool; it would be too fragile.

Chopping Board

A favorite piece of treen is a chopping board; the portable one shown on page 2607 and in Figure G can be hung on the wall when not in use. Use a 1½-by-6½-by-17-inch piece of straight-grained fir, maple, or birch for this project; pine would be too soft. If you buy the wood, its nominal thickness will be 2 inches but its actual thickness will be 1½ inches. Enlarge the pattern in Figure G, trace it on the wood, saw along the edge lines, and drill the hole in the handle. Since this wood is thick, sawing will go slowly. After sawing, rasp and sand the chopping board to the cross-sectional shape shown in Figure G.

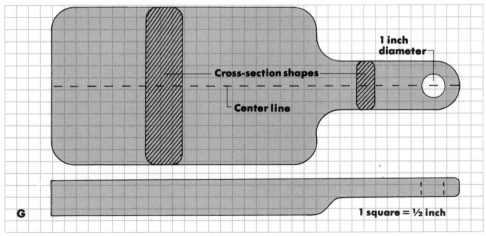

Figure G: To enlarge the chopping board pattern, draw a grid of ½-inch squares, and copy the half pattern above the center line onto the larger grid, one square at a time. Cut out the half pattern, and trace it on 1½-inch-thick wood. Flip the pattern to the other side of the center line, trace the matching half, and saw out the chopping board. Enlarge the side view of the handle; trace, and saw or rasp it to shape.

Convenient table accessories for a party are such handmade treen as this napkin holder, hors-d'oeuvre wheel, snack server, and salad set. The napkin holder and hors-d'oeuvre wheel have been left unfinished, the snack server has a cooking-oil finish, and the salad set has been given a burnt finish.

Carving and Molding
Treen for the party table

Treen can move out of the kitchen and into the dining or living room in the form of serving dishes or trays, salad bowls, and napkin holders. As the photograph above shows, they are fine conversation pieces, particularly if you have made them yourself. Salad bowls and circular serving dishes are traditionally made from a single block of wood, either with a wood-turning lathe or by laboriously hollowing them out of a solid block with a large gouge and mallet. The projects that follow, however, are designed to be made quickly with hand tools.

Napkin Holder
The napkin holder pictured above is a simple project. It was cut from a 1½-by-5-by-5½-inch block of wood (Figure H) and has a ¾-inch opening for napkins. If you want to hold more napkins, use a thicker piece of wood and make a wider opening. To make the holder, enlarge the pattern, trace it on the wood block, then follow the sequence of saw cuts suggested in Figure H. Make the first three cuts with a cross-

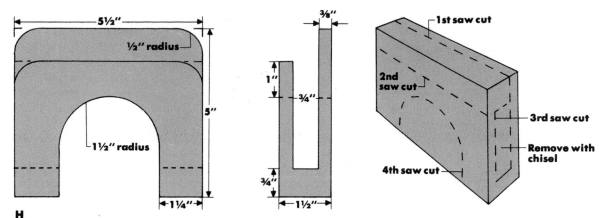

H

Figure H: Draw the lines for the saw cuts that will form the napkin holder on a 1½-by-5-by-5½-inch wood block. Then make the cuts in the sequence shown. If you want to hold more napkins, use a thicker block of wood and widen the space in the center.

cut saw, the fourth with a coping saw. Remove the waste between each edge and the semicircular cutout with a chisel and mallet. Round the top corners of the holder and sand all surfaces until they are velvety smooth. The holder may be oiled, or stained and given a varnish or lacquer finish.

Snack Server

The pretzel-filled snack server shown opposite and in Figure I is made of two pieces of wood. The top is cut from a 1½-by-9-by-12-inch block; the bottom from a ¾-by-8½-by-9-inch block. (If you want a lighter bowl, make the bottom block only ½ inch thick.) Enlarge the patterns in Figure I and then trace on the wood blocks. Drill a ½-inch starting hole just inside the line marking the inner wall of the food-holding area. Insert the coping-saw blade through this hole, and saw along the pattern line. Repeat for the piece that forms the handle of the server. Round the upper edges of this top piece with a rasp and sandpaper, but leave the edges that attach to the bottom square. Saw out the bottom piece to fit under the serving portion of the top piece; round the lower corners of the bottom piece. Apply white glue where the top and bottom pieces meet and clamp the two pieces together. Use wood scraps to keep the clamp from marring the server. Wipe off excess glue and let the joint dry thoroughly for 24 hours. Then carefully sand the joined pieces all along the seam where they meet (as shown in photograph 7).

7: To smooth some areas (in this case the snack server and its base), you will find the job easier if you wrap the sandpaper around a small piece of carpeting or some similar flexible backing.

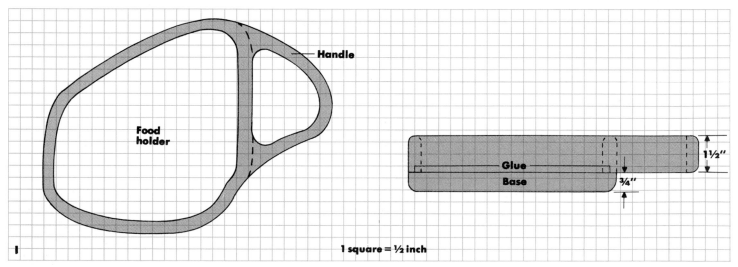

1 square = ½ inch

Figure I: To enlarge the design for this snack server, draw a grid of ½-inch squares; then copy the design onto the larger grid, one square at a time. Cut out the pattern, trace it on the wood blocks, and saw out the pieces. The base fits under the part that holds the food; the dotted lines in the top-view drawing show where the base pattern ends. Areas inside the walls of the server and its handle are sawed out after drilling starting holes.

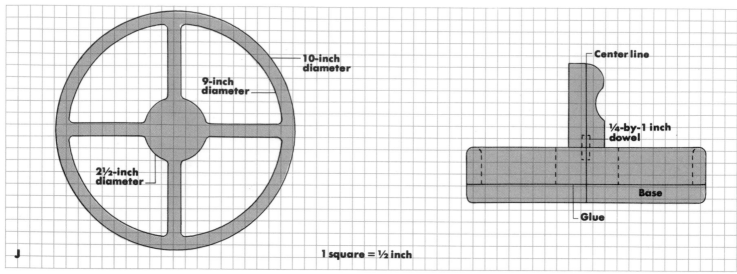

8: To cut out an enclosed area such as this ring for a salad bowl, first drill a starting hole near the edge of the area to be cut. Insert the coping-saw blade through the hole, reattach the blade to its frame, and saw.

K

Figure K: To make the salad bowl, cut out a series of six wooden circles of graduated sizes. Start with the widest circle, 11 inches in diameter, and reduce the diameter of each successive circle by ¾ inch. Draw an inner circle on each of the five top rings, ¾ inch from its edge. Then saw out the inner rings. When assembled, the rings will overhang each other and the base as above, right.

Figure J: To enlarge the pattern for the hors-d'oeuvre wheel, draw a grid of ½-inch squares and copy the design onto the larger grid, one square at a time. Cut out the pattern, trace it on the wood blocks, and saw out the pieces. Drill starting holes for the coping-saw blade in the areas separating the wheel spokes. Enlarge the pattern for the handle; trace it on 1½-inch-square stock. Saw the concave curve on all four sides, and rasp and sand all surfaces to get the shape pictured on page 2610.

Hors-d'Oeuvre Wheel

The wheel portion at the top of the hors-d'oeuvre dish (page 2610 and Figure J) is cut from a 10½-inch square block, 1½ inches thick. The base that forms the bottom of the dish is cut from a 10½-inch square block, ½ or ¾ inch thick. Enlarge the pattern for the wheel (Figure J), center it on its block, and trace the pattern of the outer and inner circles, the wheel spokes, and the hub. Then saw the outer circle. Using the same pattern, trace the circle for the base on the thinner block of wood and saw it out. Drill starting holes in each of the four areas between wheel spokes, and saw out the waste material between the spokes. Sand the inside surfaces of the wheel and round off the top edges, leaving the bottom edges square. Round off the bottom edge of the base leaving the top edge square. Figure J shows the rounding of both of these pieces.

Coat the joining surfaces of the wheel and the base with a thin film of white glue and clamp these pieces together, using wood scraps to protect the work from mars. Wipe off excess glue, and leave the pieces clamped for 24 hours so the glue can dry thoroughly.

Cut a 3½-inch length of 1½-by-1½-inch wood for the handle. Drill a ¼-inch hole, ½ inch deep in the center of one end of the handle. This will hold the dowel that will join the handle to the wheel hub (Figure J). Enlarge the pattern for the handle, trace it on the wood, and curve the handle with either a saw or rasp, then sand it to shape. Drill a ¼-inch hole, ½ inch deep, in the center of the wheel hub for the other end of the dowel. Cut a 15/16-inch length of ¼-inch dowel (1/16-inch shorter than the combined length of the holes to allow room for excess glue). Coat the dowel, the holes, and the bottom of the handle with glue. Insert the dowel into the handle and fit the handle in place on the wheel hub. Use a large C-clamp or improvise weights to hold the pieces together while the glue dries. Wipe off any of the excess glue before it hardens.

Give the dish a final sanding. Such servers are not designed to hold liquids but they can be used for damp hors-d'oeuvres if given an oil finish. If yours will be used for dry snacks only, it can be finished with stain and varnish or lacquer.

Salad Bowl Set

An easy way to make a salad bowl (page 2610) is to cut a graduated series of wood rings; then stack them so they overlap each other as shown in Figure K. The rings are joined with waterproof resorcinol glue, then are shaped with a rasp and sandpaper to make a bowl shape before the base of the bowl is attached. There will be scrap material left over, but to save material, the smallest ring can be cut from the waste area of the largest ring.

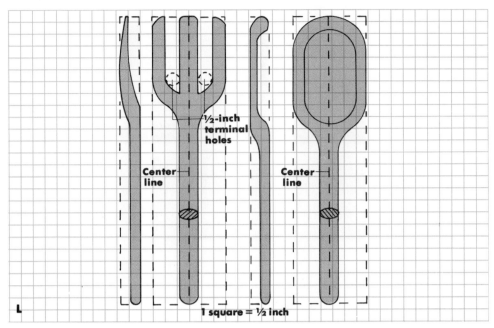

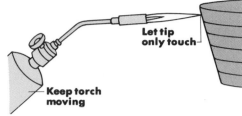

Figure M: To achieve a burnt finish, move the tip of the flame from a propane torch across the wood. This will scorch the wood just enough to make a visible burn mark. To intensify the effect, pass over the area again, but do not concentrate the heat on any one spot.

Figure L: To enlarge the patterns for the spoon and fork, draw a grid of ½-inch squares, and copy the designs onto this larger grid, one square at a time. Cut out the patterns, trace them on the wood, and saw out the pieces. Enlarge and trace the side profiles, and saw them out. The bowl of the spoon is hollowed out with a gouge.

Using a compass, draw the circles for the base and for the rings that form the bowl walls on ¾-inch-thick wood. The top ring has an outside diameter of 11 inches and an inside diameter (the line you cut to form the ring) of 9½ inches. The ring just below will have a 10¼-inch outside diameter and an 8¾-inch inside diameter. For each ring below that, reduce the diameter by ¾ inch (or the radius by ⅜ inch). The base has a 7¼-inch outside diameter.

With all circles drawn, cut along the circumference of each with a coping saw. Then drill a starting hole just inside the inner circle on each, insert the saw blade through this hole, and saw out the inner circle (photograph 8). Glue the surfaces of the rings that will touch when the five rings are stacked so that each overhangs the one below it by ⅜ inch all around (as shown on the right in Figure K). Omitting the base, stack the five rings and clamp (or place the assembly upside down under a weight). Wipe off the excess glue and leave the clamps or weight in place for 24 hours while the glue dries.

Using a rasp and sandpaper, shape the glued-together rings to the bowl contour shown on the left in Figure K. When the wall has been shaped, round off the bottom corners of the base, apply glue to the areas where the base and bowl wall meet, and clamp the wall to the base (or put the assembly under heavy weights). Wipe off excess glue and leave the assembly clamped or weighted for 24 hours.

Salad Fork and Spoon
To make the wooden fork and spoon for this set, enlarge the patterns in Figure L, trace them on wood blocks; then saw, rasp, and sand all contours except the bowl of the spoon. Hollow that out with a gouge; then sand it smooth. Rasp and sand the handles to the cross-sectional shape shown in Figure L.

Achieving a Burnt Finish
To give this salad set a burnt finish, as shown on page 2610, scorch the surface lightly and carefully with a hand-held propane torch. Keep the tip of the flame at a distance that will produce a barely visible burn mark (Figure M). Keep the flame moving, passing over the same area several times if necessary to achieve the desired effect. (Practice on scrap wood first.) A similar effect can be achieved with a candle flame but it will take much longer. After burning, sand and dust each piece and then give them a cooking-oil finish.

For related projects and crafts, see "Folk Art," "Sculpture," and "Totem Poles."

TRELLISES
Climbing Greenery

For plants that need something to grow on—and people who like to watch them—trellises are the answer. There are many kinds. You can make a fan-shaped trellis small enough for a flower pot, or large enough to decorate a fence (page 2617). You can make a trellis that turns an ordinary doorway into an inviting entrance (opposite). You can move a freestanding trellis outdoors in summer and indoors in winter, to have foliage and flowers close at hand all year (page 2619). And you can use such a trellis to screen out an unattractive view.

In its simplest form, a trellis is a latticework of wooden strips, often in a frame, to which plants can cling. Climbing roses, sweet peas, and wisteria were favorite trellis plants in old-fashioned gardens. Modern gardeners use trellises with a wider variety of plants, including such vegetables as pole beans, peas, and tomatoes. Some simple trellis patterns are shown in Figure A. The latticework can be arranged to form squares, diamonds, plaids, or basket-weave effects; sections can be set close to each other to block wind or screen an unsightly view, or apart to admit air and light.

For latticework, ¼-by-1-inch strips of lath work well. These you can nail or screw to each other and to 1-inch-square framing strips. Parts of the frame that overlap can be notched to half thickness providing a flat surface for attaching the lattice strips. Or you can sandwich the latticework ends between framing pieces. Bolt the trellis frames to steel fence posts or creosote-treated 2-inch-square wood posts pointed at one end, driven at least 8 inches into the ground (12 to 18 inches if the trellis is large and heavy). Assemble the latticework in easy-to-handle sections. Frame these sections; then drive posts and attach the frames to them.

These are the basics of simple trellis construction. The fan, freestanding, and doorway trellises shown on pages that follow call for somewhat more elaborate building techniques. But all can be made from stock lumber with common hand tools. However, some of the parts are assembled with wooden dowels, a rustproof form of joinery.

Tools you will need include: crosscut saw; coping saw; coarse-toothed ripsaw or saber saw with medium-coarse blades; square; straightedge; protractor; screwdriver; hammer; chisel; measuring tape; drill with bits of the sizes specified; vise; several large C-clamps; rasp; sandpaper; and pencil. The lumber, fasteners, finishes, and other special materials needed are listed with each project.

Opposite: With a leafy cover of ivy growing across the top lattice and shelves holding potted coleus, chrysanthemum, marigold, parsley, and wandering jew, this trellis makes an inviting entryway.

Figure A: At right, top to bottom, are some standard patterns for trellis latticework. Below are trellises of sticks, wire, and lumber for supporting a climbing vegetable such as a tomato or cucumber growing in a pot or in the garden.

Frank Kommer learned woodworking as an apprentice in his uncle's cabinetry shop in Locust Valley, New York. After attending college, he had a variety of construction jobs, including building a house heated by solar energy. He established his own woodworking shop in East Hampton, Long Island, where he builds furniture that he also designs.

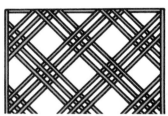

Basket weave

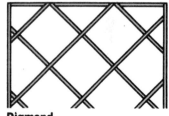

Diamond

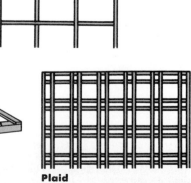

Square

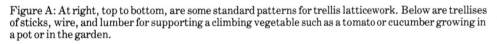

Sticks — **Tie or glue**

Concrete reinforcing wire

Tomato trellises

Cucumber trellis

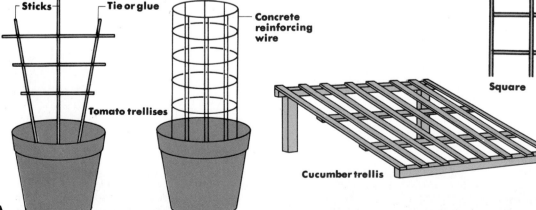

Plaid

A

1: Divide the width of the fan-trellis board into 5/16-inch segments; then use a straightedge to draw lines marking these segments from the base line to the trellis top.

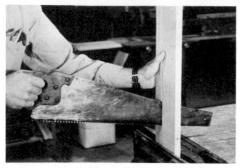

2: With the board in a vise, saw along the vertical lines to make the fan-trellis strips, ending each saw cut at the base line.

3: Drill a ⅜-inch dowel hole ½ inch below the base line, halfway through from one side, then halfway through from the other. If you measure carefully, holes will meet in the center.

4: Cut a 5½-inch length of ⅜-inch dowel and tap it through the hole you have drilled for the reinforcing peg designed to keep the base from splitting when the fan is spread. No glue is needed if the base is soaked.

Greenery and Growing Things
Fan trellises

Fan-shaped trellises such as the one shown opposite are easy-to-make plant supports. One variation, the double-fan shape shown on page 2618, can stand on its own as a lawn ornament.

A fan trellis can be any size you want. The one detailed in Figure B is 3 feet tall. It is made from a single board, cut part way through to make vertical strips that are then spread into a fan shape. To make a miniature version for a flower pot, use thinner wood of a length and width that seem in scale with the size of the pot. To enlarge the fan trellis, use lumber of the same thickness as in Figure B, but increase the width and length as well as the length of the wooden spike that holds the trellis upright.

For the size shown, choose a 3-foot-long piece of 1-by-6-inch pine (the actual dimensions will be ¾ by 5½ inches). Pick a piece with straight grain and no knots to reduce the danger of splitting. Draw a base line across the board 6 inches from one end; this will be the limit line for the vertical saw cuts. Divide this line into 5/16-inch segments. Mark identical segments near the top end of the trellis board. Use a straightedge to connect corresponding segment marks (photograph 1). With the

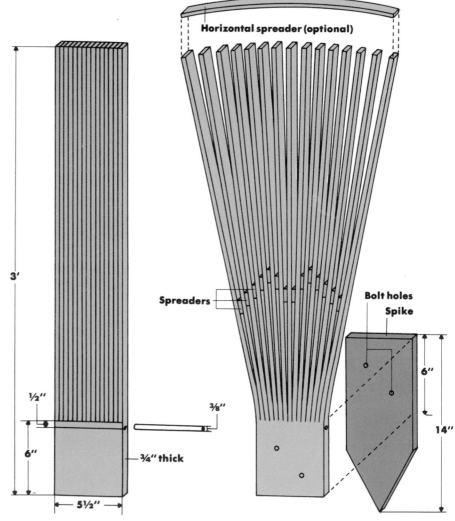

B

Figure B: The fan trellis is cut from a single board, sawed in 5/16-inch-wide strips from the top to a point 6 inches from the bottom (left). The dowel strengthens the base and helps prevent splitting. The strips are soaked in water to make them flexible, then are spread into a fan shape with spreaders (right). The pointed wood spike will be driven into the ground to support the trellis.

base of the trellis board clamped in a vise, use a ripsaw or saber saw to cut along the lines, from the top of the board to the base line (photograph 2). Work from one edge of the board to the other as you make these cuts.

Draw another squared-off line across the board ½ inch below the base line. Extend this line across each edge of the board, and mark the center point on each edge. Then, with the board horizontal in the vise, drill into each center point half-way through the board, using a ⅜-inch bit (photograph 3). If you can keep the bit at right angles to the board's edge, the holes will meet in the center of the board.

Cut a 5½-inch length of ⅜-inch dowel and tap it through the hole you have just drilled (photograph 4). This will minimize the chance of the base splitting when the strips are spread later.

Soak the Wood
Soak the cut trellis in water for several days, until the strips seem pliable enough to be spread into a fan shape. You can place the trellis in a partially filled bathtub and weight it down, or you can soak it in a water-filled garbage can. If the trellis is longer than the can, turn it end for end occasionally.

Inserting the Spreaders
To spread the strips into a fan shape, I used small pieces of ¼-by-¾-inch wood lath, cut to 1-inch lengths. The spreaders may be inserted in a straight line across the trellis (photograph 5), or may be worked into a design (photograph 6). Starting about halfway down the trellis, insert spreaders between the outer strips first, working from each side toward the center. Use the eraser end of a pencil to nudge them into position.

If the wood seems about to split if you add another spreader, stop work and resoak the trellis with the spreaders in place for another day or so. If you want to spread the strips into a wide fan, as on page 2618, drive 1½-inch-long screws through the outer strips, 1½ inches above the end of the saw cuts on each side, to prevent splitting. For appearance, you can add a second line of spreaders higher up on the trellis, as in the fan on page 2618. If there is not enough tension to hold them in place, fix each in position with waterproof resorcinol glue.

I like to leave the top of a fan trellis open, but some fan trellises are topped with a single strip that forms a curved spreader (Figure B). To add such a strip to this trellis, use a measuring tape to determine the length needed and cut a ¼-by-¾-inch wood strip to this length. Soak the strip in water for several days until it can be bent over the top of the spread trellis. Then, starting in the center, nail the top strip to each vertical strip with galvanized or plated ¾-inch brads.

5: Insert spreaders between the strips, working from the outside edges toward the center. You can use the eraser end of a pencil as a tool to work the spreaders into position.

6: Spreaders may be positioned to form a decorative pattern like this, or they may be placed in an arc or a straight line across the fan. Work out the design you find most pleasing.

A fan trellis, with a fire thorn plant being trained to grow on it, adds landscaping interest when set against the vertical lines of a tall wooden fence. Such a trellis may be staked to the ground or supported by a large pot of soil.

Making the Spike

Cut a 14-inch-long piece of 1-by-6 (actual dimensions ¾ by 5½ inches) for the pointed wooden spike that will hold the trellis upright (Figure B, page 2616). (The spike for a 3-foot fan trellis should be driven 8 inches deep; that for a 5- or 6-foot trellis or a double-fan trellis should be driven 12 inches deep.) Cut one end of the spike to a point. In the other end drill holes for the two 1¼-inch No. 8 flathead wood screws or two 1¾-inch No. 8 or No. 10 stove bolts that fasten the spikes to the base of the trellis (Figure B, page 2616). Then drive the spike in the ground, and screw or bolt the trellis to it.

Let the soaked trellis get thoroughly dry before applying a finish. Erase all pencil marks, and smooth with medium, then fine sandpaper. Then coat the wood with clear preservative and let it weather. For a deeper color, you can use stain and several coats of varnish, with the wood preservative or creosote used only on the spike. I used stain and varnish on the trellises shown.

Double-Fan Trellis

The double-fan trellis shown at left and in Figure C has a third dimension that adds to its design interest. It consists of two fan trellises, one of them being sawed in two so it can join the other at right angles. You will need: two 3-foot lengths of 1-by-6; three 5½-inch lengths of ⅜-inch dowel; a 14-inch length of 1-by-6 for the spike; and small pieces of wood lath for the spreaders. Lay out the two fan trellises and saw the strips as previously described. Mark one trellis *a* and the other *b*. On trellis *a*, drill a ⅜-inch dowel hole ½ inch below the base line as before, and tap a 5½-inch length of ⅜-inch dowel into this hole. On trellis *b*, square off a line across the board 1 inch below the saw-cut limit line, and drill a dowel hole at this point. Then mark and drill a second dowel hole 1¼ inch up from the bottom (Figure C). Do not insert these dowels. Soak both trellises and insert the spreaders as previously described.

To make a double-fan trellis, cut two fan trellises; then saw one of them in half and join the two halves to opposite sides of the uncut trellis.

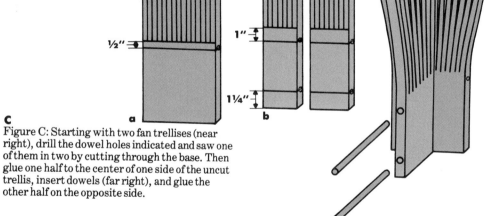

C

½"

1"

1¼"

a

b

Figure C: Starting with two fan trellises (near right), drill the dowel holes indicated and saw one of them in two by cutting through the base. Then glue one half to the center of one side of the uncut trellis, insert dowels (far right), and glue the other half on the opposite side.

Joining the Trellises

After the wood of both trellises has dried, draw a vertical line through the base of trellis *b* so that eight segments are on one side and seven segments are on the other. Saw that trellis apart along this line. Coat one of the edges with waterproof glue, and clamp this half of trellis *b* to trellis *a*, making sure it is centered and at right angles to trellis *a*. Using the holes already drilled in trellis *b* as guides, extend them through trellis *a*. Tap 5½-inch lengths of ⅜-inch dowel through the holes so that they protrude on the opposite side of trellis *a*. Coat the cut edge of the remaining half of trellis *b* with waterproof glue; then fit that piece over the protruding pegs. Clamp tightly until the glue dries. Drive two 1½-inch No. 8 wood screws through each outer strip of the two trellises, locating them 1½ inches and 3 inches above the line marking the bottom of the saw cuts; these strengthen the structure. For the wood spike, cut an 18-inch length of 1-by-6 and point one end as before. Cut a ¾-by-6-inch slot in the center of the other end of the spike, so that the spike will fit against trellis *a* and around one half of trellis *b*. Screw or bolt the spike to the trellis. After sanding, finish with clear wood preservative, or with a coat of stain and several coats of varnish.

Greenery and Growing Things
Freestanding trellis

A portable plant-display trellis that you can use outdoors or indoors, or place anywhere to screen an unsightly view, needs to be freestanding. On the unit shown below, climbing plants will grow up the back; the dowel shelf in front will hold potted plants or a rectangular plant box.

To make this trellis, you will need two 5½-foot lengths of 2-by-4 (actual dimensions 1½ by 3½ inches) for the uprights, two 13-inch lengths of 2-by-4 for the shelf arms, two 16-inch lengths of 4-by-4 (actual dimensions 3½ by 3½ inches) for the feet, one 35-inch length of 2-by-6 (actual dimensions 1½ by 5½ inches) for the

When brought indoors for the winter, a freestanding trellis makes a decorative front-hall accessory. This one has German ivy climbing up the back trellis and pots of pink impatiens and wandering jew set on the front shelf.

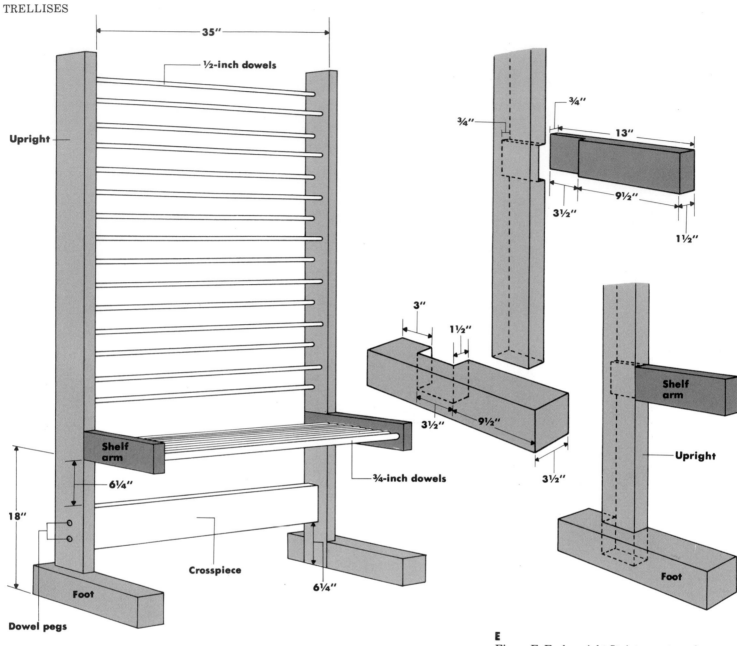

35"

½-inch dowels

Upright

Shelf arm

6¼"

18"

Dowel pegs

Foot

Crosspiece

6¼"

¾-inch dowels

3"

1½"

3½"

9½"

3½"

¾"

¾"

13"

9½"

3½"

1½"

Shelf arm

Upright

Foot

D
Figure D: A perspective view of the freestanding trellis shows how it is assembled. Shelf arms and feet project forward an equal amount to insure stability when pots are set on the shelf.

E
Figure E: Each upright fits into a rectangular notch cut in the inside of each foot. Where a shelf arm joins an upright, both are notched to half width and then glued together.

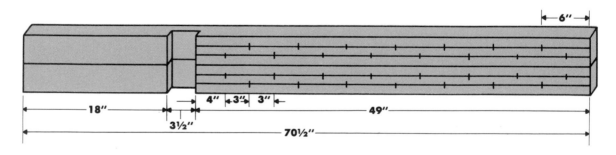

6"

18"

3½"

4" 3" 3"

49"

70½"

F
Figure F: After you cut slots in the uprights for the shelf arms, clamp the uprights together and mark them for staggered ½-inch dowel holes at 3-inch intervals between the notches and the top of each upright.

crosspiece, ten 3-foot lengths of ¾-inch dowel, fifteen 3-foot lengths of ½-inch dowel, and four 3-inch lengths of ½-inch dowel.

Each upright fits into a cutout in a foot piece (Figures D and E and photograph 7). Measure 3 inches in from the back of each foot piece and draw the cutout, first squaring off lines across the top, the inside surface, and the bottom of the foot. Working from these lines toward the front of each foot, outline a 1½-inch-deep 3½-inch-wide cutout on the inside of each foot. The uprights will fit into these cutouts (as shown in Figure E).

Making the Cutouts

Square off lines across the inside face of each upright 18 inches up from the bottom. These will mark the lower end of the ¾-by-3½-inch cutouts made in the uprights for the shelf arms. To fit these cutouts, one end of each shelf arm must be cut to half (¾-inch) thickness and to a width of 3½ inches. Use a square to mark the ¾-by-3½-inch cuts to be made in the ends of the shelf arms.

To make the cutouts you have marked, saw just inside the pencil lines marking the edges of each cutout to the line marking the depth of the cutout. To remove the wood between these cuts, make additional saw cuts every ¼ to ⅜ inch between the edge cuts. Then clean out the wood with a sharp chisel to the line marking the depth of the notch. Rasp and sand the cut areas smooth.

Drilling the Dowel Holes

Clamp a shelf arm to the work table with the cutout area face down. Draw a center line the length of the arm. Starting 3½ inches from the end that has been cut out, mark ten 1-inch intervals. Drill ¾-inch holes ½ inch deep at each mark. (Wrap tape around the drill bit ½ inch from the tip as a depth guide.) Make corresponding holes in the second shelf arm the same way.

Clamp the uprights together with the cutouts facing up. Draw lines dividing each upright face into thirds, from the cutout to the top of the upright (Figure F). Starting 3 inches from the top, make marks at 3-inch intervals arranged in a staggered line down each upright, as shown in Figure F. Fit a ½-inch bit in the drill, wrap a piece of tape ½ inch from the tip to serve as a depth guide; then drill holes ½ inch deep at each mark.

Fitting the Joints

Coat all cutouts and the areas of the frame members that will join them with waterproof resorcinol glue. Then fit the uprights to the feet and the side arms to the uprights (photograph 7). Clamp for eight hours until the glue dries. Sand both assemblies with successively finer sandpaper, starting with 60 grit and ending with 120 grit, always rubbing with the grain.

The 35-inch crosspiece fits between the two uprights (Figure D). Mark its position centered on each upright, 6¼ inches below the shelf arm and 6¼ inches above the bottom of the foot. To attach the crosspiece, drill two ½-inch holes for dowels in each upright and corresponding holes in each end of the crosspiece.

Assembling the Trellis

Lay one section of trellis on the worktable with the dowel holes facing up. Put waterproof glue in each dowel hole and insert the dowels, pressing each snugly into its hole (photograph 8). Insert the two ⅜-by-3-inch dowels that will hold one end of the crosspiece in place, apply glue to one end of the crosspiece and the exposed end of the dowels, and fit the crosspiece onto its dowels and against the upright. Then, with a helper, turn the section of trellis with the inserted dowel holes in it upright, and brace it against a wall.

Put glue into all of the dowel holes in the second trellis side and the exposed end of the crosspiece, and fit this section onto the dowels already glued in place in the first section. Glue and tap in the two remaining dowels that hold the other end of the crosspiece. Wipe off any excess glue with a damp cloth. Wedge the assembly as tightly together as you can, perhaps between a wall and your workbench, for at least eight hours. Finish the trellis with clear wood preservative or with stain followed by several coats of varnish.

7: Glue the matching shelf arms and uprights together; then glue the bottom of each upright to its foot. Holes have been drilled to receive shelf dowels as well as those between the uprights.

8: After ½-inch dowels have been glued into the holes in one upright, put glue into the shelf holes and glue ¾-inch dowels in place.

The same doorway is shown with the trellis installed (above) and before the trellis was built and installed (below).

Greenery and Growing Things
Doorway trellis

The photographs at left and on page 2614 show what a trellis can do to make a doorway seem more inviting. In keeping with the rustic look of the weathered shingles, I used construction-grade fir, left dowel ends exposed, and stained the trellis dark brown. The shelves provide a place for potted plants that can be changed with the season, tulips in the spring, geraniums and petunias in the summer, and chrysanthemums until late fall. Since the door is not far from the kitchen, I usually have a few pots of herbs on the shelves as well.

To make this trellis, you need the materials listed opposite. Start by making the deep rectangular cutouts in the top of each upright post (Figures G and H). The horizontal crosspieces will fit into these cutouts forming what is called a bridle joint. Draw a center line dividing the width of the top of each upright post, and extend this line 4½ inches down each side. Draw lines across the top and down the sides 1¼ inches on either side of the center line, using a square to keep them at right angles to the top. Square off a line across the upright post 4½ inches from the top on either side. Drill ½-inch holes just inside in the two corners where the lines marking the sides and the bottom of the cutout meet. Use a ripsaw or saber saw to cut just inside the side lines of the cutout from the top to the bottom line. Then insert a coping-saw blade into one hole, and saw across the bottom line to the other hole (photograph 9). Rasp or chisel the corners square.

Notches called rabbets are made in the two crosspieces so they will fit down into the slots in the upright posts and lock there (Figure H). Square off lines 6 inches and 8½ inches from both ends of each crosspiece extending these lines across the edge and the sides of the crosspieces. These lines will be the sides of the rabbet cut into the crosspiece. Draw lines joining the two side lines 1 inch in from the edge of the crosspiece and mark the area to be cut out with Xs. Remove the waste material by drilling holes in the corners where the lines meet, sawing down the side lines, and then sawing across the bottom line to complete the cutout. Rasp or chisel the corners square.

Square off a line on the underside of each end of each crosspiece 5 inches from the end, and draw diagonal lines from these points to the upper corner of each crosspiece (Figure H). Saw along these diagonal lines (photograph 10). Square off the width and thickness of an upright post on the inside corners of each shelf (photograph 11 and Figure I). Hold a square or straightedge along the line marking the length of this cutout, and mark where the square intersects the opposite side of the

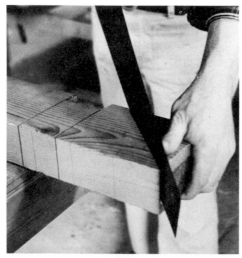

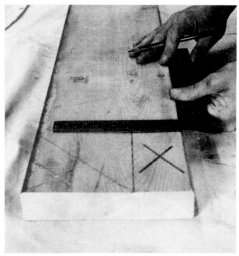

9: To make the cutouts in the top of each upright post, mark them and drill holes where the side and bottom lines meet. Saw down the side marks, then use a coping saw to cut across from one hole to the other. Rasp or chisel the corners square.

10: After making the rabbet cutout for the upright post on each crosspiece, form the back sloping ends of the crosspiece by sawing on a diagonal line from the top corner of the crosspiece down to within 1 inch of the cutout on the underside.

11: On each inside corner of each shelf, mark a cutout that is as long and wide as the upright post the shelf will fit around. Draw a diagonal line from the edge of this cutout to a point 5½ inches in from the edge of the shelf on the opposite side.

Brace

82½″

Crosspieces

Lattice slats

Brace

Upright posts

Shelves

96″

36″

15″

15″

18″

G

Figure G: A perspective view of the doorway trellis shows how its parts are assembled.

Materials list, doorway trellis (actual sizes)

Four pieces of fir, 2½ by 5½ by 96 inches (upright posts)

Two pieces of fir, 2½ by 5½ by 82½ inches (crosspieces)

Six pieces of fir, 1½ by 7¼ by 36 inches (shelves)

Two pieces of fir, 2½ by 3½ by 36 inches (wood braces)

17 white-pine slats, ¾ by 2½ by 38 inches (top lattice)

32 pieces of ½-inch dowel, each 4½ inches long

Four 6-inch lengths of ¾-inch dowel

Four dowel wedges

Three dozen 6-penny nails for slats

8 feet of string

Two 90-degree metal angle braces

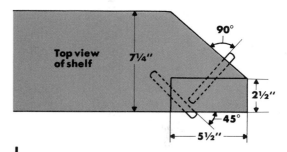

Top view of shelf 7¼″ 90° 2½″ 45° 5½″

I

Figure I: To fasten the end of a shelf to an upright post, use dowels driven at the angles and to the depths shown.

Diagonal cut

Crosspiece

1″ 5½″ 1″ 2½″ 5″ 2½″

5½″ 1½″ 1½″ 4½″

2½″ 2½″

Upright

H

Figure H: Each crosspiece fits into a slot cut in each upright and is notched so that it locks in place on the upright. Diagonal line (left) shows cut to be made on the end of the crosspiece (right).

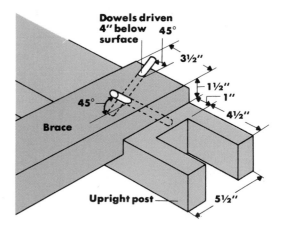

Dowels driven 4″ below surface 45° 3½″ 1½″ 1″ 4½″ 45°

Brace

Upright post 5½″

J

Figure J: To fasten one end of a brace to an upright post, use dowels driven at the angles and to the depths shown.

shelf. Draw a diagonal line from this mark to the point where the cutout intersects the edge of the shelf. Saw the cutout and along the diagonal line (photograph 12).

The two braces at the top of the trellis are cut out to fit over an upright post on each side, and their outer corners are cut or beveled at 45-degree angles (Figures J, page 2623, and K). Mark and saw the cutouts and cut the bevels.

Assembling the Trellis

Lay the upright posts in pairs on the ground close to where the trellis will stand. You will assemble one side of the trellis first, then the other, then join the two sides with the crosspieces. Fit the bottom and top shelves under the upright posts and the middle shelf on top of the posts (photograph 13) following the placement and spacing of the shelves given in Figure G, page 2623. If you have or can borrow two bar clamps, use them to clamp the two posts together (photograph 14). If not, brace the sides with weights such as cement blocks. If you use the clamps, fit scraps of wood between clamp and post to keep from marring the post. Fit the brace between the uprights and 1 inch below the cutout at the top of each post on either side.

With the posts, shelves, and brace well clamped or braced, fit your drill with a ½-inch bit and wrap tape around the bit 4 inches from the tip to serve as a depth gauge (photograph 14). Then drill the holes for the dowel pegs, following the locations in Figure L and the dowel angles and depths in Figures I and J. Before tapping in the dowels, bevel the edges on both ends slightly with a rasp or sandpaper. This will make them easier to drive and help prevent splitting. When you tap in the dowels, you can leave about ½ inch protruding on either side for a rustic appearance.

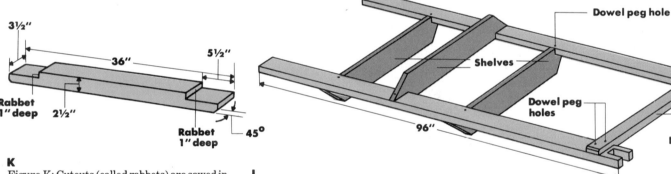

K
Figure K: Cutouts (called rabbets) are sawed in each end of each brace so they fit over the upright posts when assembled.

L
Figure L: This is how the two uprights, the three shelves, and the brace that make up one side of the trellis are assembled. Note the locations of the dowel fasteners.

12: On each outside corner of each shelf, saw along the diagonal line from a point 5½ inches in from the outside edge to the edge of the cutout on the inside of the shelf. These cuts give each shelf an attractive, tapered edge.

13: With a pair of uprights laid parallel on the ground, fit the shelves in place. Locate the brace over the uprights so that it is 1 inch below the bridle joint cutout that was made in the top of each upright.

14: With a wood brace clamped firmly to the upright posts, and the bit marked with tape 4 inches from its tip, drill dowel holes through the brace into the upright at the angles shown here and in Figure J, page 2623.

Attaching the Crosspieces

With both sides of the trellis assembled and ready for joining, lay them on their edges, and fit the crosspieces in the cutout bridle joints at the top of each upright post. Fit the drill with a ¾-inch bit and drill a hole through each upright post (photograph 15) stopping at the point where the tip of the drill starts to break through the wood. Remove the drill and complete the hole by drilling up from below; this keeps the wood from splitting.

Place the ¾-by-6-inch dowels in a vise, and make thin saw cuts down the center of each end about 1½ inches deep. Bevel the edges of each dowel end. Drive the dowels in place through the bridle joint (photograph 16). Let them protrude ½ inch on either side. Drive thin wedges of wood into the saw cuts in each dowel. These wedges, together with the expansion of the wood when it gets wet, will lock the upright and crosspiece together. Tilt the trellis up, slide sawhorses under it, and attach the second crosspiece to its bridle joint as you did the first.

Making the Trellis Top

The lattice that forms the trellis top is made of seventeen ¾-by-2½-by-38-inch white-pine slats. If the trellis will fit flat against a wall, the 2-inch overhang of these slats will be in the front and the protruding ends of the rear dowels should be cut off flush. If there is space and you prefer it, you can divide the 2-inch overhang of the slats so that 1 inch is in front and the other inch is in back. Nail a slat across each end of each crosspiece. Drive a nail into the end of each of these two slats, and tie a string between the two nails to serve as a guideline (photograph 17). Nail the remaining slats so their ends are even with this string, starting at one end and allowing one slatted space (2½ inches) between slats. Use two 6-penny nails, staggered, to fasten each end of each slat to a crosspiece.

Tilt the trellis completely upright into position, and give it a suitable finish of clear wood preservative or, if you want it dark like mine, a dark-brown stain followed by several coats of varnish. If the trellis will stand in a windy place you can cut circular holes in the shelves into which the potted plants can be fitted. To attach the trellis to the house, use two 90-degree angle braces. Fasten one side of each brace to the outside of each upright, two-thirds of the way up from the base of the upright. Fasten the other side of the brace to the house. Coat the metal braces with rustproofing paint to keep them from corroding.

For related crafts and projects, see "Greenhouse Construction" and "Lighted Indoor Gardens."

15: Fit the crosspiece into its cutout in the upright and, holding the bit perpendicular to the upright, drill through until the point of the bit starts to break through the wood. Complete the hole by drilling from the other side.

16: After slotting the center of each dowel and beveling the edges on each end, tap it into the dowel hole through the upright and the crosspiece until it protrudes ½ inch on the other side. Drive thin wooden wedges into the dowel slots.

17: With a string guide marking the distance each slat should extend beyond the crosspiece, nail each slat to each crosspiece with two 6-penny nails in each end of each slat. Allow the space of one slat between each pair of slats.

TROPICAL FISH

In the Swim

An aquarium is a glass tank designed to house fish, but plants, sand, and other objects are often arranged within the tank so the fish can be displayed to best advantage. Aquariums such as the one shown opposite are commonplace today, but it was only with the opening of the first public aquarium at the Zoological Gardens, Regent's Park, London, in 1853, that glass tanks became popular. Before then fish were kept in ponds or containers ranging from clay pots to punchbowls. The main advantage of the shallow rectangular glass tank is that its surface area allows a maximum amount of oxygen from the air to enter the water to keep the fish healthy. Too, the glass makes visible the underwater world.

Some 4,500 years ago, the ancient Sumerians were the first to keep fish, stocking ponds with freshwater varieties as a source of readily available food. The Chinese first made a science of pisciculture (fish keeping). During the Sung Dynasty (960-1278) they changed the greenish-brown color of carp through selective breeding to develop the world's most admired fish, the goldfish. These were often placed in elaborate porcelain vessels for viewing.

The Romans, too, were fish keepers. The mullet, a saltwater fish that can survive in fresh water, was a favorite. Wealthy Romans also kept moray eels in ponds, despite their snakelike appearance and razor-sharp teeth; no banquet was complete without a platter of eel, considered a great delicacy. During the Middle Ages, fish keeping all but disappeared except in the monasteries. Early in the fifteenth century, a monk named Dom Pinchom artificially fertilized and incubated fish eggs, but his discovery was unknown elsewhere until his manuscripts were published in 1850.

It was the display in Regent's Park zoo that initiated a worldwide fish-collecting craze. At the beginning of this century, only a few varieties of tropical fish were available for home aquariums, but the hobby grew rapidly until more than 1,500 species were available to the home aquarist.

Robert S. Mathews (left) had an aquarium when he was a child. That led him to study biology and natural history at Princeton University. After he received a master's degree in zoology at Columbia University, he traveled around the world with research expeditions. He then returned to New York to become curator of the tropical fish department at the New York Aquarium in Battery Park. Bob has also been associate editor of Collier's Encyclopedia and has taught mathematics and science at Baldwin High School, New York.

Walter Johanson (right), a professional photographer, became interested in small saltwater fish when he first went scuba diving near Cozumel, Mexico. Since then he has developed new techniques for building and photographing aquariums like the ones shown on these pages. Walter lives in New York in a loft that also houses his photography studio.

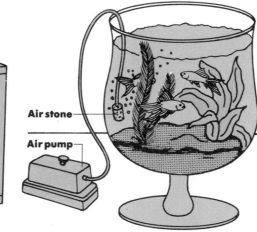

A
Figure A: A rectangular tank shape offers a large surface area to permit the free exchange of oxygen and carbon dioxide that is necessary for the respiration of fish. But only a few fish can be kept healthy unless some supplemental means of aerating the water is provided.

Air stone

Air pump

B
Figure B: To keep fish healthy in a fish bowl, a bubbler should be added. This is a tube with a porous air stone at one end, through which air is pumped. The air stone disperses a continuous stream of tiny air bubbles to add oxygen to the water. Air comes from an outside pump.

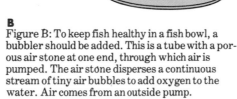

Many freshwater specimens from South America occupy this community tank. Among the easiest to see are the large spotted fish at left, the *Geophagus juripari*; the albino fishes at far left, the *Cichlasoma severem*; and the thin striped fish at center, *Anostomus anostomus*.

Red-fin sharks (*Labeo erythrurus*) are freshwater fish marked with a dark tan body and bright red fins. They feed on decaying matter; so they are useful for keeping a tank clean. At maturity, they reach 6 inches in length. Red-fin sharks should be kept in 75-to-85-degree water with a neutral pH.

The rosy fish with puckered lips at right is a kissing gourami (*Helostoma rudulfi*). Two kissers in a tank provide amorous displays when their lips meet. As adults they are about 10 inches long. Kissers should be kept in 78-to-85-degree water with a pH between 6.4 and 7.2. Kissers feed daily on algae and live or frozen food. The spotted fishes at left are relatives of the kissing gourami, the pearl gourami.

This is a pair of peaceful discus (*Sympsodon aequifasciata haraldi*). A discus' body is thin and round; it reaches about 8 inches in diameter at maturity. When a discus is frightened, the iridescent blue shading its body becomes darker. This helps it hide in foliage or rocks. The discus needs 75-to-85-degree water with an acid-to-neutral pH of 6.2 to 7. They prefer live food such as white worms and brine shrimp.

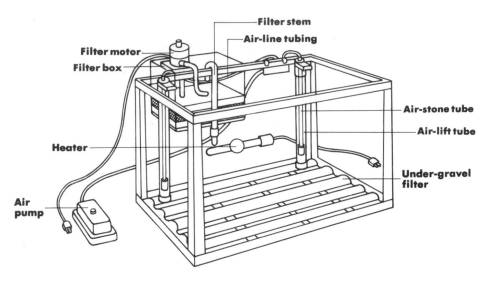

C

Figure C: A double filtration system will aerate the aquarium water, adding oxygen as well as cleaning it. The under-gravel filter at the bottom of a tank draws water through a bed of gravel, where bacteria convert wastes into food for aquarium plants. The filter's two vertical tubes are connected with an air pump outside the aquarium (left). The second filter is in a box hooked on the back edge of the tank. In it are two fiber filter pads with charcoal between them. A separate motor is in the filter box, connected to the tank with a hooked spout.

Saltwater or Freshwater Fish

Tropical fish sold by aquarium dealers have been transported thousands of miles from their natural habitats. They fall into two major categories, those that live in fresh water and those that require salt water. Pages that follow describe aquariums for either kind of fish. But I advise a beginner to set up a freshwater tank first. It is easier to maintain and requires less equipment; moreover, freshwater fish are less expensive than those for a marine tank, indicating they are easier to propagate and keep healthy. Once you can easily maintain a freshwater tank, you may elect to change to a saltwater aquarium or have both kinds of tanks. The switch would not be difficult; many of the materials used in a freshwater tank can also be used in a marine aquarium.

Assembling an Aquarium

Before you decide what size and type of tank to buy, try to imagine its finished appearance. When outfitted and illuminated, an aquarium can be the focal point of any room. The tank should not interfere with household activities, but visibility is critical. If the tank is placed where the fish go unnoticed, interest will wane quickly.

There are practical considerations, too. A full tank is very heavy and must have adequate support. (One cubic foot of water weighs 62 pounds, or about ten pounds per gallon.) The tank must be level; an uneven surface will put a slight twist in it that could cause a leak. Some tanks come with stands, but you can set a tank on any level surface that is strong enough. Once filled, the tank should not be moved. Changes in water temperature are hazardous to tropical fish. If the room temperature is not constant (75 to 78 degrees for most fish), you will need an aquarium heater, so the tank will need to be near an electric outlet. The tank should not be placed in direct sunlight; it causes unsightly algae to multiply rapidly.

I suggest that you buy the largest tank you can afford and a stand to hold it. It should have a capacity of at least ten gallons, a cover, and a built-in reflector designed to hold two 25-watt fluorescent tubes. (Fluorescent tubes are cooler than incandescent bulbs.) In addition, you will need these materials for cleaning and filling a tank; a drop cloth; bicarbonate of soda; sponge; paper towels; a 5-foot-long plastic hose, ½ inch in diameter; and two gallon-sized plastic buckets. To plant the tank you will need: two pounds of medium-grained aquarium gravel for each gallon of water; a one-quart measure; noniodized table salt; potassium permanganate; and a 9-by-12-inch glass container. For maintaining the tank you will need: pH test kit; thermometer; ¼-inch hollow plastic siphon tube longer than the tank is deep; a fine nylon net; a scraper; and an empty five-gallon can. Contrary to popular belief, fish can live in a tank for many years without gravel, plants, heater, filter, or aerator, as long as the tank is not overcrowded. But if you plan to have more than a few fish, you will need a filter to keep the water clean and aerated, an air pump to operate the filter, and a heater with thermostatic control.

Preparing the Tank

Initially, set the tank in its permanent location, and cover the floor under it with a drop cloth or plastic. Pour lukewarm water in the tank to a depth of 4 inches and add two tablespoons of bicarbonate of soda or salt. (Buckets that have contained soap or detergent should not be used to fill a tank.) Swish the water around, and wipe the tank inside and out with a sponge. Scoop out the cleaning solution and rinse the tank. Check the tank for leaks; stainless steel joints can be patched with aquarium cement, but mend glass seams with silicone rubber cement.

Environment Controls

To keep aquarium fish healthy, three environmental controls are needed: the water must contain enough oxygen at all times so the fish do not suffocate, it must be kept clean, and it must be maintained at a constant temperature. For an aquarium that will house a number of varieties of tropical fish, I recommend that these controls be achieved with a double filtration system plus a thermostatically controlled heater, as shown in Figure C, opposite, and in photographs 1 through 9. (In the event of a power failure, of course, the fish could quickly die if emergency measures are not taken. Inexpensive battery-operated pumps are available for such occasions.) Insofar as the oxygen supply is concerned, there is a constant interchange between the surface of the water and the air above. So a few fish could live in an aquarium tank without supplemental aeration. As the fish population increases, however, so does the hazard of suffocation; a sure warning that the danger point is near comes when fish are observed near the top of the tank, seeming to gulp the oxygen-laden water they find there. Simply circulating the water, as any filtration system does, increases the oxygen exchange. Even more effective is to force incoming air from the filter's air pump through a porous block called an air stone; myriad tiny bubbles result, speeding the oxygenation of the water. Circulation and aeration also speed the dispersal of the carbon dioxide which the fish exhale, which otherwise could be hazardous even when enough oxygen is present.

Keeping the tank water clean and fresh smelling is important to the health of the fish. An under-gravel filter at the bottom of the tank draws water through a layer of gravel, and at the same time draws wastes and leftover bits of food into the gravel. There, bacteria convert these potentially harmful materials into nitrogen compounds that will feed the aquarium plants. Such plants, while they create a more attractive aquarium, cannot be used to balance the aquarium environment as was long believed. The plants do indeed take in carbon dioxide and give off oxygen—but only during daylight hours, when photosynthesis is in progress. At night, the respiration of the plants involves taking in oxygen and giving off carbon dioxide, adding to the need for mechanical aeration.

In addition to the under-gravel filter, I suggest an outside filter hooked on the back of the tank as the most effective way to clean water near the top of the tank. Also useful is a plastic tube that you can use with fingertip suction to remove visible bits of debris from the tank after each feeding.

To assemble this combination, first place the under-gravel filter on the bottom of the empty tank with the openings for the two air-lift tubes at the back corners. Fit an air-lift tube into each opening (photograph 1), and put a thin tube containing the porous air stone inside each air-lift tube. The rate of circulation of the water is controlled by the depth of the air stone in the air-lift tube; the deeper the air stone, the greater the flow.

Next, cover the under-gravel filter with clean aquarium gravel or glass chips to a depth not exceeding 2 inches (photograph 2). This will provide the bed for rooting aquarium plants.

Connect the top of each air-lift tube to a plastic valve with three openings (a three-gang valve), hooked on the back of the tank near one side. Make the connection with plastic tubing cut to fit (photograph 3, page 2630). Leave one valve open at the end

1: Place the under-gravel filter on the bottom of the empty tank, with the two air-lift-tube openings at the back corners of the tank. Slip one end of each air-lift tube into its hole so it stands erect. Then put each smaller air-stone tube inside an air-lift tube, with the air-stone pads at the bottom. The deeper the air-stone pad is set in the air-lift tube, the greater will be the flow of water through the filter.

2: Gravel is poured on the under-gravel filter to a depth of 2 inches. Unless the gravel has been prepared for aquarium use, rinse it in a bucket with running water from a hose. If you prefer, you can use colored glass chips instead of gravel.

3: A plastic three-gang valve (see also photograph 4) is hooked onto the back edge of the tank. Connect each air-lift tube to a valve opening with a piece of plastic air-line tubing. Leave the valve nearest a corner of the tank open to release air.

4: To complete the installation of the under-gravel filter, use plastic tubing to connect the center opening of the valve with the opening on the portable air pump that remains outside the tank (Figure C, page 2628).

5: To line the filter box, hook it temporarily on the front edge of the tank. Put the filter tray in the filter box with its stem opening on top. Make sure that the filter stem lines up with the tank corner when it is placed at the rear.

6: Cover the filter tray with a filter fiber pad, fitting the hole in the pad over the filter-tray stem. Cover the pad with charcoal chips, spreading them evenly over the padding to a depth of 1 inch. Put a second pad on top of the charcoal bed.

of its top edge to release air. Connect the valve opening at the base of the three-gang valve with the motor-driven air pump (photograph 4). This tubing must be long enough to reach wherever the air pump will be placed outside the tank. When the tank is filled and the air pump plugged in, the under-gravel filter will operate.

Outside Power Filter System

You may need to add an outside power filter if you anticipate a substantial fish population. As there are many brands of power filters to choose from, follow the assembly instructions on the package. The power filter shown here locks into a tray at the bottom of a filter box. To assemble a filter of this type with ease, hook the filter box temporarily on the front of the tank and insert the filter tray (photograph 5). Be sure the stem of the tray is on top and positioned so it will be near a corner of the tank when the box is moved to the back.

On top of the tray, place a 1½-inch-thick piece of filter fiber, fitting the hole in it over the stem of the filter tray. Pour a 1-inch layer of charcoal chips into the box (photograph 6). Then add a second piece of filter fiber. Move the box to the back of the tank, next to the valve of the under-gravel filter. Hook the motor housing onto the stem of the filter tray, with it sitting on top of the box (photograph 7). You can fit the tubing for the separate under-gravel filter between the box and the tank. Finally, hook the curved ends of two or three cone-shaped filter stems over the rim of the filter box with the long ends extending into the tank (photograph 8).

Heaters

If you have a room where the temperature is maintained at a constant 70 degrees Fahrenheit, you can keep the tank water at the recommended 75 to 78 degrees with two 25-watt incandescent bulbs inserted in reflectors. Incandescent bulbs produce heat as well as light, so you would need to turn off the lights during a heat wave. That might leave the aquarium plants without the light they require. Instead, I recommend using cool fluorescent tubes as a light source and a heater for maintaining uniform temperature. If there is a substantial difference in temperature between day and night, a heater becomes indispensable. There are many to choose from; a thermostatically controlled heater that fits inside the tank with suction cups to stick it vertically or horizontally to the glass is convenient (photograph 9). The glass tube containing the heating element comes in contact with the water; the warmed water rises, setting up a current independent of the filter system. When the heater is plugged in after the tank has been filled, the thermostat switches the heater off and on to hold the water at the desired temperature. Heaters that hang vertically with the electric connection out of the water are safer, especially as they get older, but they must be used in conjunction with forced circulation of water to maintain an even temperature through the tank.

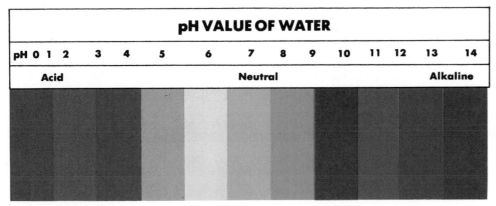

pH VALUE OF WATER

pH	0	1	2	3	4	5	6	7	8	9	10	11	12	13	14

Acid	Neutral	Alkaline

D

Figure D: The acidity or alkalinity of a sample of water can be tested with dye that comes in a pH test kit. The solution will turn to a color that can be compared with the numbers and colors on this scale. Water that registers between 7.0 and 7.2 is neutral and does not need to be adjusted unless the particular species of fish that you plan to keep requires a different pH. (See fish table, pages 2636 and 2637.) If the color indicates the water is too acid, less than 7 on the pH scale, gradually add sodium bicarbonate to the tank water or filter box until the water is made neutral. If there are fish in the tank, give them time to adjust to the change by making sure you do not change the pH more than .2 points in 24 hours. If the water is too alkaline, more than 7.2 on the pH scale, add sodium biphosphate the same way.

Readying the Tank

With the aquarium assembled, there are still a number of steps to take before you introduce the fish. You must condition the water, fill the tank, test the equipment, and do the planting before you put in any fish. Anything that goes into the tank should be clean and, except for the fish and the plants, made of chemically inert materials.

Rainwater and pond water are likely to be too polluted for use in an aquarium. Tap water that is safe for human consumption can be used if chemicals such as chlorine or fluorine are allowed to disperse and hard water salts such as calcium and magnesium are removed. In addition, a basic freshwater community tank will require a relatively neutral water, neither acid (a pH test under 7.0) or alkaline (a pH above 7.2, Figure D, above). It is rarely necessary to alter the pH of tap water, but water too acid can be corrected with sodium bicarbonate, water too alkaline with sodium biphosphate. Both are available at aquarium stores; follow package instructions. Some freshwater tropicals prefer a wider pH. For specific recommendations, refer to the freshwater fish chart on pages 2636 and 2637.

Surprisingly, once fish and plants have inhabited tap water for a time, it becomes conditioned by the inhabitants. But at the beginning, precautions should be taken to make the tap water as safe as possible. To remove chlorine, fluorine, or calcium bicarbonate from tap water, simply let the water stand in an open tank for 24 hours. The harmful gases will be dispersed through the surface. Excessively hard water is harder to correct. To determine whether you have hard water, try to make a lather with ordinary soap. If the lather is not rich, the water is hard. (You can also obtain information about the local water supply from aquarium dealers, the water department, or the local board of health.) To remove salts from hard water, you can boil it in a large pot. Let the water cool; then use only the top half for the aquarium. You can also filter the water through a special filter, available at tropical fish stores, chemical suppliers, and some garages. Such a filtering device is likely to be more economical than buying distilled water at a drugstore. (At least once a month, siphon and replace one quarter of the old tank water with fresh tap water to maintain the acid-alkaline balance.)

If you are going to put plants in your aquarium, fill it only halfway at first. Use a small pail (if you are using boiled water) or a plastic hose that will reach from the tap to the tank (if you have soft water). There are two ways to fill the tank without disturbing the gravel. One is to cover the gravel with a thin sheet of clear plastic. Then gently pour the water on the plastic and remove the sheet as it floats to the top. The other is to set a cup on the bottom of the tank and pour water gently into the cup. Let the water overflow and remove the cup when the water level reaches its rim. Smooth the gravel surface with the palm of your hand.

7: Hook the assembled filter box on the rear of the tank next to the valve. Make sure the stem of the filter truly is next to the tank corner. Sandwich tubing between the tank and the filter box. Rest the pump on the box near the tank corner. Position the pump with its spout over the tank and the electrical cord behind the filter box. Add an extension cord to the wire if it does not reach the nearest outlet.

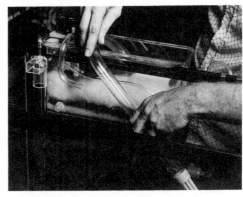

8: To complete the outside filter assembly, add from one to three hooked air stems with the short end in the filter box and the long end in the tank. Once the tank is filled, use fingertip suction to fill each filter stem with tank water. Then hook each stem over the filter box and remove your finger to siphon water from the tank through the filter.

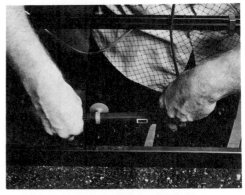

9: Center a thermostatically controlled heater inside the tank so its rubber suction cups hold it on the back wall of the tank. Check the condition of the heater periodically; a worn connection or a damaged cord is hazardous.

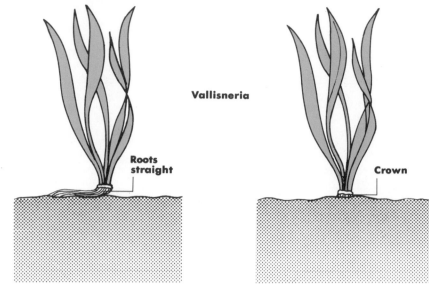

E

Figure E: To plant an aquatic, gently drag its roots through the gravel to separate them. Then cover the roots with gravel, leaving the root crown just above the surface.

This tank was landscaped with a variety of live and artificial plants. A tall stalk of ambulia (far left) and the cardamine plant next to it (with round ruffled leaves) were planted near the back of the tank. In the center of the tank is an Amazon sword plant with sprawling leaves; at far right is a pigmy chain sword. Squat plants such as tape grass and a dwarf sagittaria were placed near the front of the tank. The fish swimming in the tank include a pair of marble-veil angels (*Pterophyllum scalare*) at right, a school of neon tetras *Hyphessobrycon innesi*) at left, and a kissing gourami (*Helostoma rudolfi*) barely visible behind the tip of the cardamine plant.

Planting Aquatics

Although fish can survive without plants, the plants serve several important functions in a freshwater tank. They make the aquarium more interesting to look at, they reduce the multiplication of algae, and they supply food for the fish indirectly by promoting the growth of various organisms. Plants also shelter small fry from attacks and provide egg nests.

A vast number of floating and rooted plants are available for a freshwater aquarium. A few are shown opposite. I do not recommend that you collect wild plants; they can introduce undesirable parasites. Before you put any plant in an aquarium, sterilize it by placing it in a container filled with warm water. Add noniodized table salt until the water tastes salty, and add potassium permanganate until the water is a red-wine color. Let the plant soak for ten minutes.

Aquarium plants are of two types: bunch plants, which can be floated or planted, and runner plants, which must be planted. Floaters provide shelter for young fish and trap fish eggs like a net. With runner plants, the trick is to get them rooted in your tank. They often come with strips of lead twisted about the roots as an anchor; such weights should be removed as lead salts are toxic to fish. A small rock or pebble can be used instead for anchoring a plant. But avoid limestone, including coral and seashells, and metal-bearing rocks, as they will dissolve in time and turn the water hard. Rinse any rock that will be used in a solution of bicarbonate of soda before placing it in the tank. Artificial plants will neither benefit nor harm the fish; they are carefree decorations that can be installed easily.

The way you landscape the tank is purely aesthetic. Some plants look better in clumps, while others can stand alone. For a panoramic effect, plant the back corners of the tank in a U shape. This leaves the front of the tank open as a swimming area where the fish are easy to view. If the tank is to be viewed from both sides, arrange the plants in triangular shapes tapering from the ends of the tank and meeting in the center. A large, leafy plant can stand alone in the center of a tank.

Position the plants with your fingers or a pair of tongs. Slide the plant through the gravel to separate the roots. Then cover the roots with gravel, leaving the crown exposed (Figure E). Tropical fish stores carry plant fertilizers that can be added to the water to keep plants healthy without harming the fish.

There are hundreds of tank accessories available—divers, shipwrecks, caves, castles, and mermaids among them. But any natural objects, such as a few stones among the plants, can provide the fish with a place to hide.

With planting complete, fill the tank with water to the bottom of the top edging strip so you do not see the top of the water. If the tank is new, a small oil slick may form on top of the water. Blot up the oil with a paper towel. Then plug in the filter pumps and the heater to make sure that they are working properly. Submerge each filter system entirely below the water level and cover the opening at the curved end with a forefinger. When the tube is filled with water, replace the stem over the inner edge of the filter box and remove your finger. If the water doesn't siphon the

CRAFTNOTES: AQUATIC PLANTS FOR A FRESHWATER AQUARIUM

The aquatic plants described below are readily available at most tropical fish stores. Bunch plants can be planted or simply floated in the aquarium water. But once a bunch plant takes root and displays new shoots, you can take a cutting by snipping off a shoot with a knife or scissors. Float this shoot or plant it in sand in a jar of water. When the cutting develops hairlike roots, plant it in the gravel of your aquarium. Plants that produce runners, such as the Amazon sword plant, can also be started from cuttings. Some plants that are more expensive, such as the Madagascar lace plant, are started from seed. To do this, roll each seed in a pellet of mud and bury it in the aquarium gravel. Avoid carnivorous plants such as utricularia or bladderwort as they may eat fish fry.

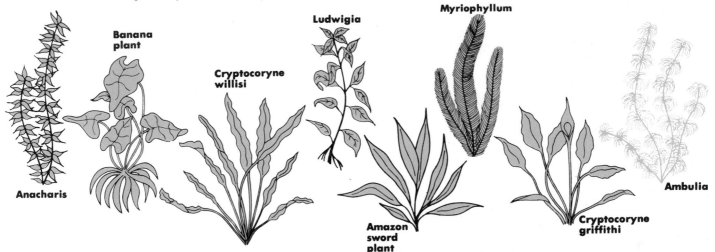

Banana plant · Ludwigia · Myriophyllum · Cryptocoryne willisi · Anacharis · Amazon sword plant · Cryptocoryne griffithi · Ambulia

Bunch plants

Ambulia, a light-green plant with spidery, tasseled leaves, is useful for landscaping an aquarium because it provides a soft contrast with the leaves of more sharply defined plants.

Anacharis, a sturdy plant with graceful, waving stalks and tiny leaves, is available in either dwarf or giant varieties.

Bacopa is a hearty plant with bright-green, rounded leaves that ascend a stiff stem in pairs. Bacopa does not bloom when it is submerged; so propagation must be done with cuttings. Bacopa grows best in water 64 to 68 degrees Fahrenheit.

Cabomba or **fanwort**, a light-green plant with fanlike leaves, resembles a plume. Its wispy leaves shelter small fish, but the leaves are thin and do not encourage spawning. Cut off 2 inches of the top before planting to forestall decay.

Cardamine is a plant with ruffled leaves of a pale-green color. It is a good oxygenator.

Hygrophila, a plant with oval-shaped, light-green leaves, is useful for landscaping the back or sides of a tank. To propagate it, take cuttings below a stem node that displays root tendrils. Hygrophila requires daylight and a water temperature between 70 and 80 degrees.

Ludwigia natans or **floating ludwigia** has green, arrow-shaped leaves that are red underneath. Ludwigia can be easily propagated by cutting a piece of the plant where leaves join the stem. Ludwigia needs abundant light.

Moneywort is a vertical climbing plant with abundant shield-shaped leaves.

Myriophyllum or **water milfoil** has fine fernlike leaves that somewhat resemble a raccoon's tail. When planted in clusters, it provides an ideal place for spawning. Myriophyllum requires water no warmer than 75 degrees.

Runner plants

Amazon sword plant has two distinct forms, one with narrow leaves, the other with broad leaves. As the flower stalk produces new shoots, it becomes quite full, making this a good plant for center display. Amazon sword plants flourish in water kept above 70 degrees.

Aponegeton crispus has long, light-green, ripple-edged leaves. As the leaves of this plant may reach a length of 12 inches and a width of 3 inches, they need space to unfold. This plant does well in warm water, about 75 degrees.

Banana plant has leaves that resemble a cluster of bananas. It can be floated in a tank or planted.

Cryptocoryne cordata has long leaves that are olive green on top with red undersides. It should be planted in water kept between 70 and 80 degrees.

Cryptocoryne griffithi, a long-rooted plant, has broad, dark-green leaves that are brown underneath. It is a sturdy plant that can survive rough treatment.

Cryptocoryne willisi has thin, wavy-edged leaves that are a bright medium-green. This plant can be propagated with its short runners or by taking a cutting from the parent plant. Once rooted, do not move the plant.

Dwarf sagittaria is a small plant with tapered leaves used for frontal planting.

Hornwort, a dark-green floating plant, has bristly leaves like the branches of a pine tree. It is useful in a breeding tank.

Madagascar dwarf lily is a decorative plant that bears pale-blue flowers above the water.

Octopus plant has about a dozen long strands. It is moplike and somewhat resembles an inverted octopus.

Rooted hairgrass is dense-growing grass with hairlike leaves from 4 to 6 inches long.

Sagittaria sinensis has broad leaves; often two or three are planted in a clump to make a center group.

Underwater palm is a miniature aquatic that resembles a palm tree.

Vallisneria is a small plant with ribbonlike leaves. A dozen or more can be planted in a single tank.

Vallisneria torta has long, tapered leaves that are twisted like a corkscrew.

Water sprite is a fernlike plant with several stems.

Water orchid, a vinelike plant, has thick, heavy roots like those of an orchid. It is quite ornamental.

Wisteria is a single-stemmed plant that has fernlike leaves.

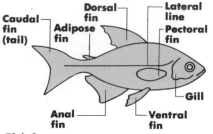

Caudal fin (tail) · Dorsal fin · Adipose fin · Lateral line · Pectoral fin · Gill · Anal fin · Ventral fin

Fish features

By familiarizing yourself with the external features of a fish, you will be able to recognize changes that warn you of disease or malfunctioning equipment. The mouth, nostrils, and eyes are located on the head of the fish. Gill slits on each side of the throat are openings through which breathing occurs. In some fish, the gill covers act as propellers in addition to the caudal fin, the main drive fin.

Most of the body surface is covered with scales. The fish secretes slime over these scales to protect it against bacteria and fungus. Netting fish can injure this slime coating Any nets used should be of the finest nylon mesh. Once a fish has been netted, it may not eat for several days. Fish have a special organ known as the lateral line, a series of pores running from the gill cover to the tail. This system responds to low-frequency vibration. It keeps a school of fish together at night, and probably enables a blind fish to locate food.

tank water to the filter box, repeat this procedure in the same way, until the water flows properly.

The Tank Cover

A tank cover keeps fish from jumping out, reduces evaporation, and keeps the water cleaner. It also shields the fish from curious dogs and cats. The cover can be a commercial one with sockets for incandescent bulbs or fluorescent tubes. Or it can be simply a piece of glass that projects over three edges, allowing space at the rear for the filter tubes and heater cord. But if the tank is covered too tightly, an excess amount of carbon dioxide can build up. To release the carbon dioxide, leave half the tank uncovered for several hours each day, and circulate the water.

Before putting fish in the tank, make sure the heater is working properly. Set the thermostat at 75 to 78 degrees (10 degrees cooler if you plan to have goldfish), place a thermometer in the tank, and read the water temperature several times a day to check the thermostat's accuracy.

Selecting Freshwater Fish

Several factors enter into the selection of fish for a single aquarium tank—how much money you have to spend (the less expensive fish are likely to be easier to care for); what kind of fish appeal to you; the size of the fish in relation to the space within the tank; the water temperature and pH required by the fish. Your goal will be to establish a community in which several species can live harmoniously. This is not difficult if you select fish that will be about the same size at maturity. Of course, in any group there may be a bully who nips the fins of others and is a general nuisance. If this happens, banish the bully.

To begin, stock the tank with only one pair of fish. As long as you have about 1 square foot of surface area per inch of fish, the water should not require supplemental aeration. Introduce additional fish gradually, selecting species compatible in size and environmental requirements (see Craftnotes, pages 2636 and 2637). Choose some that will prefer the upper levels of the tank, others that favor lower levels. Once you have a substantial fish population, or several large fish, keep the air pump turned on all of the time.

Some fish, the live-bearers, produce their young alive. They will eat these fry, but if the vegetation is thick enough, the young can hide from the older fish and survive. If you want to raise the young, purchase a breeding trap, a container separated from the tank by a perforated divider. The pregnant female is placed at an upper level so when the fry is born, it will drop to safety in the bottom of the container. Any of the live-bearers are suitable for a freshwater aquarium.

You can mix live-bearers with another group of fish, the egg-layers. (A dozen egg layers are shown on page 2637.) The female deposits eggs in the tank and the male fertilizes them. There are a large number of egg-layers, among them the tetras that come in a great array of colors. Some tetras of the neon variety seem to glow in the dark; the barbs form another large group. *Tetrazona*, popularly known as tiger barbs, tend to be scrappy, but they are active and decorative. Gouramis, larger than the others, are generally peaceful but some tend to hide. Corydoris, a South American catfish group, live near the bottom, cleaning food off the gravel.

If your tank is large, you will want larger fish. The cichlid family, which includes the angelfish and the discus, has many interesting varieties. Another group of fish called anabantids has a spectacular member, the Siamese fighting fish. They are available in bright reds, greens, and blues, and some have milky bodies with colored fins. The males all fight with each other, and should be kept separately.

Homecoming

Most pet stores put tropical fish in a water-filled plastic bag or other container for transport. If the temperature remains constant, the fish are in no danger. The best way to put the fish in a tank is to float the sealed container in the tank for about 20 minutes. Then feed any fish already in the aquarium and turn off the tank lights. Add 1 teaspoon of a specially prepared fish remedy for each 5 gallons of water to lower the bacteria count, making it less likely for the newcomer to contract a disease. Open the container and gently pour a cupful of tank water into the container; then spill off some of the water. Repeat this procedure several times until the pH of the tank water and container water are equal. Then lay the container on its side and allow the fish to swim out. To capture a fish, use two nets of the same size. Hold one net stationary as you direct the fish into it with the other.

Feeding

Overfeeding is one of the principal reasons aquarium fish die. Fish are cold-blooded so they do not need to maintain body temperature. They need far less food than a warm blooded animal. Fish should be fed twice daily at a regular time with an amount of food they can eat in five minutes. Fry need larger amounts of food.

Pet stores, supermarkets, and fish stores stock a variety of dry, live, and frozen food. Dry foods are usually a combination of shrimp, salmon eggs, liver meal, and spinach. Formulas differ; so use several brands in rotation for variety, or mix some cod-liver oil with the dry food to provide a wide nutrient base. With dry food, sprinkle a tiny bit in the tank and watch the fish feed. If they eat avidly, give them a tiny bit more. When they seem to be feeding in a leisurely manner, stop.

Live foods provide the best nutrition for fish, especially if you want them to breed. Live food can be put in a special feeder that will permit the food to escape into the tank. Tubifex are slender red worms found in slow muddy streams. Daphne and its relatives are water fleas, available live or frozen. Brine shrimp, too, can be purchased alive or frozen. Packaged brine-shrimp eggs, available at fish pet shops, can be hatched by following package directions. Pet shops often sell mosquito larvae which are excellent food, but mosquitoes have a way of hatching and are not welcome around the house.

When you vacation, fish are no problem. Adult fish of small breeds can go for two weeks without food. Feed the fish a normal amount at the usual time before you depart and when you return home. You will be tempted to make the latter feeding larger than normal, but don't. Automatic feeders or vacation food blocks that dissolve gradually to keep from fouling the tank are also available at pet shops.

Maintaining the Tank

If the water gets cloudy or foul smelling, the tank needs cleaning. The easiest way is to siphon some of the water into a bucket, and let the dirt settle; then slowly decant the clean water on top back into the tank. Or make a simple filter by plugging a funnel loosely with a scrap of cloth. Use a wire to hang the funnel on the edge of the tank; then filter the water back into the tank. If you keep a reserve of conditioned water, you can replace one-fourth of the tank water once a week.

The growth of algae must be kept under control. Algae lodge on plants and tank walls. Green algae will flourish if there is too much light, brown algae if there is too little. Remove algae from plants by rubbing their leaves and stems with your fingertips. Use an unsoaped steel-wool pad or a scraper to clean algae off the glass.

Even with an air pump, when the air temperature reaches the nineties, the fish will gasp for oxygen. To lower the water temperature, put several ice cubes in a closed jar and float the container in the tank. Watch the temperature of the tank water to make sure it does not go too low.

Diseases

Before you add new fish to the tank, place them in quarantine for about a week for observation, to make sure they do not transmit disease to healthy fish. Hang a beaker with a wide mouth on an edge of the tank, with the rim just above the water. Fill the beaker and put the new fish in it.

The easiest way to tell that something has gone wrong in an aquarium is to observe the fish carefully. Changes in color, behavior, or physical features suggest sickness. Check equipment first to make sure it is functioning properly. If the fish has difficulty swimming, it may have a chill caused by an inoperative heater. If a fish is constipated, displaying a trail of excreta, a pinch of epsom salts in the tank can alleviate its discomfort. Less often, a fish catches an infectious disease or is attacked by fungus, indicated if scales appear flaky or if gills and fins are damaged; fungus may appear as white spots on the fish's body. Most fish stores carry packaged medicines that have proven successful in treating disease.

Little is known about the life-span of fish in the wild. Some complete their life cycle in two or three months, leaving eggs to hatch with the next rainfall. In aquariums, most of the fish listed on pages 2636 and 2637 will live at least two years, and some may survive for ten.

Bibliography of freshwater fish

Aquarium Fishes by James W. Atz. The Viking Press, Inc., New York, N.Y.

Exotic Aquarium Fishes by William T. Innes. E.P. Dutton & Co., Inc., New York, N.Y.

Tropical Fish for Beginners by H.R. Axelrod. Tropical Fish Hobby Publishing House, Neptune City, New Jersey.

Tropical Fish Handbook Catalog by Aquarium Stock Company, New York, N. Y.

Tropical Freshwater Aquaria by Peter Bird and George Cust. Bantam Books, Inc., New York, N.Y.

Bibliography of marine fish

Atlantic Reef Corals by F.G. Walton Smith. University of Miami Press, Coral Gables, Fla.

Exotic Marine Fishes by Dr. Herbert R. Axelrod and Dr. Cliff W. Emmens. Tropical Fish Publishing House, Neptune City, New Jersey.

Fish and Invertebrate Culture by Stephen Spotte. John Wiley and Sons, Somerset, New Jersey.

Marine Aquarium Keeping by Stephen Spotte. John Wiley and Sons, Somerset, New Jersey.

Pacific Marine Fishes and Saltwater Aquarium Fishes by H.R. Axelrod and W. Burgess. Tropical Fish Publishing House, Neptune City, New Jersey.

Saltwater Aquarium Manual by Dr. Robert Valenti. Aquarium Stock Company, New York, N.Y.

CRAFTNOTES: TROPICAL FISH

One dozen each of the most popular live-bearing and egg-laying tropical fish are included in this selection, recommended for a home freshwater aquarium. You will find a much larger variety at a tropical fish store. In each case, the scientific name of the fish is given after the common name, since a fish may have more than one common name. The illustrations and information regarding the characteristics of each fish will help you combine varieties that will live together harmoniously. Pay particular attention to unusual needs—in temperature, water pH, or food. These are essential for the fish's survival.

Live-bearers are the easier to breed. Extra feeding is all that is needed to ensure the regular production of broods. The fry are born in an advanced state of development, ready to eat and swim vigorously. Live-bearers are carnivorous; they sometimes eat their newborn to control their population. Inbreeding among live-bearers produces many color variations, but features vary only slightly, most noticeably at the dorsal and tail fins.

Most fish reproduce by laying eggs, and of these, all but a very few practice external fertilization. Some egg-layers scatter their eggs freely or fasten them on plants or stones; others carry the eggs in their mouths or deposit them in bubble nests. As a result of both crossbreeding and mutation, the vast group of egg-layers includes fish of many unusual colors and body features.

The live-bearers

The veil-tail guppy (Lebistes reticulatus) is an active fish with a delta-shaped tail that flares out as the fish swims. Males come in many colors, but females have gray bodies with colored markings and a long, black, veil-tail. Males grow 1½ inches long, females slightly larger. The veil-tail guppy needs water at 74 to 78 degrees, neutral pH of 6.8 to 7.2, and frequent feedings of prepared, live, or frozen food.

The three-quarter black delta guppy (Lebistes reticulatus) has a black body with red fins. This guppy has a wide tail. It needs a temperature of 74 to 78 degrees, a neutral pH of 6.8 to 7.2, and any kind of fish food.

The scarftail guppy (Lebistes reticulatus) has a tail that may be longer than its body. The male comes in various colors and is slightly smaller than the dull-colored female. Water should be maintained at 74 to 78 degrees, with a neutral pH of 6.8 to 7.2. The scarftail guppy will eat dry, live, or frozen food.

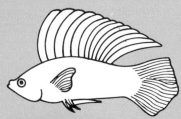

The giant sailfin molly (Mollienesia velifera) has an iridescent body with a high, wide dorsal fin edged in orange. It grows to about 5 inches in length. This fish should be kept in warm water, 78 to 84 degrees, with a slightly alkaline pH of 7 to 7.2. Giant sailfins eat algae, and bits of vegetables, and meat.

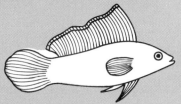

The jet-black molly (Mollienesia latpinna) has an iridescent sheen. Males have a high, broad dorsal fin with rows of red, brown, and green dots. Males reach 4 inches in length, while females grow to 5 inches. Black mollies like water at 78 to 84 degrees and a salty, slightly alkaline pH of between 7 and 7.2. They will eat all types of food, but feed them chopped green vegetables occasionally.

The Yucatan molly (Mollienesia shenops) is bred to be solid black in color, but it is also available in gray or black with orange markings. Yucatan mollies with a pointed nose and round fins grow 2 to 4 inches in length. They need warm water, 78 to 84 degrees, and a slightly alkaline pH of 7 to 7.2. They will eat crustaceans, brine shrimp, or vegetable matter.

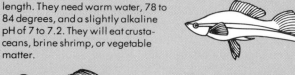

The hybrid platy (Xiphophorus) has a rich red, white or gold body with contrasting black spots. A small, hardy fish, it requires water heated to 80 degrees, with a slightly alkaline pH of 7 to 7.2. It needs a varied diet.

The red-wag platy (Xiphophorus) has a deep-red body with black fins and tail. It grows no longer than 3 inches. It should be kept in water heated to 70 to 80 degrees, with a slightly alkaline pH of 7 to 7.2. This fish eats any fish food.

The blood-red platy (Xiphophorus) is a showy tropical fish. Male and female are a rich red color. Females grow to about 3 inches in length, males are slightly smaller. Blood-red platys should be kept in a well-lit tank in water heated to 70 to 80 degrees, with a slightly alkaline pH of 7 to 7.2. They eat algae, dry food, brine shrimp, and chopped clams.

The green swordtail (Xiphophorus helleri) has a green, iridescent body with a bright red or orange stripe running from eye to tail. In the wild, the green swordtail grows to 5 inches in length, but this size is rarely seen in fish shops. The fish needs water heated to 70 to 80 degrees, with a slightly alkaline pH of 7 to 7.2. It accepts all kinds of fish food.

The red-eyed swordtail (Xiphophorus helleri) has a pink body with red eyes. It will be comfortable in water heated to 70 to 80 degrees, with a slightly alkaline pH of 7 to 7.2. Vary its diet with dry, live, or frozen food.

The red-wag swordtail (Xiphophorus helleri) has a long, red body with a black dorsal fin and tail. Like other swordtails, the red wag needs water heated to 70 to 80 degrees, a slightly alkaline pH of 7 to 7.2, and a varied diet.

FOR A FRESH-WATER AQUARIUM

The egg-layers

The lyretail panchax (Aphyosemion australe) is a carp with teeth that enable it to eat smaller species. It is a small fish, only 2 inches long at maturity. The lyretail has a chocolate-brown body decorated with carmine-colored spots and streaks. Male lyretails have large fins edged with purple and trimmed with white. These hardy fish should be kept in water heated to 75 to 82 degrees, with a slightly acid pH of 6.4 to 6.8. They favor live food such as worms or brine shrimp.

The oranda goldfish (Carassium auratus), with a large head and long, flowing fins, is a bully of the carp family. Orandas come in many colors, including red, calico, white with red caps, chocolate brown, and steel blue. Adult size can range from 3 to 6 inches in length. Orandas can withstand a wide range of pH, from 6.6 to 7.4, and temperatures ranging from 50 to 85 degrees. They eat dry, live, or frozen food.

The zebra danio (Brachydanio rerio) has a yellow body with silver and blue stripes. The popular zebras are small fish, only 2 inches in length at maturity, but they are active and need plenty of room for swimming. Zebras favor a pH range of 6.6 to 7.2, with water temperatures from 50 to 85 degrees. They eat dry and live food.

The white-cloud-mountain minnow (Tanicthys albonubes) is a fish from the streams of White Cloud Mountain in China. A peaceful fish that swims in schools, it has a green back, a green iridescent stripe on top, and a brownish-red stripe on the bottom of its body. White-clouds are about 1½ inches long at maturity. They like water temperatures of 65 to 70 degrees, with a pH range from 6.6 to 7.2. They eat dried or live food.

The harlequin rasbora (Rasbora heteromorpha) is reddish-brown on the back and front of its body. It is deep red at the rear and has a black triangular-shaped marking along its side. The harlequin rasbora swims in schools and grows to about 2 inches in length. This fish likes slightly acid water, with a pH from 6.6 to 7, at a temperature of 76 to 80 degrees. It will eat dried, live, or frozen food.

The tiger barb (Capoeta tetrazona) has a tan body, marked with black bars, and a red tail and fins. This fish should be kept in schools of five as this lessens its nipping tendency. It is 2 inches in length at maturity. The tiger barb likes a temperature of 70 to 85 degrees, with a slightly acid pH between 6.4 and 7. It eats dry or live food.

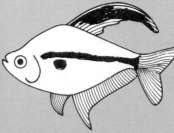

The bleeding-heart tetra (Hyphessobrycon rubrostigma) is a beautiful member of the carp family with an adipose fin. This fish has light-brown sides with a bluish glint. The anal fin is white at its base and is edged in black. The dorsal fin is pink, with a large black spot. A blood-red spot is located in the center of its body. Very spirited, the bleeding-heart tetra likes a slightly acid pH of 6.6 to 7, and a temperature between 74 and 78 degrees. It likes live or frozen food, but will eat dry food if it is hungry.

The neon tetra (Hyphessobrycon innesi) has a dark back with a brilliant green iridescent stripe from its eye to the adipose fin. It is blood-red in color from its belly to the tail. Neon tetras grow to 1½ inches in length and swim in schools. They thrive in 76-degree water with a slightly acid pH of 6.4 to 7. They eat finely ground dried food and live food in small quantities.

The marble-veil angel (Pterophyllum scalare) belongs to a family of graceful, gaily colored fishes called cichlids. This fish has a thin, round, silver body with black markings and long fins. As angelfish grow rather large, about 5 inches in length and 6 inches from top to bottom of the fins, pairs of angels that are compatible for breeding are sometimes placed in a separate tank at maturity to encourage successful fertilization. Marble-veil angels need slightly acid water, with a pH between 6.4 and 7, heated to 74 degrees. They eat freeze-dried or live food.

The South American catfish (Corydoris julii) is a bottom feeder; it eats leftover food scraps, algae, and dead material that might otherwise foul the tank. This fish has a silver-gray body with black spots. The spots give way to wavy lines on the head, gill plates, and dorsal fin. The catfish grows to about 2 inches long at maturity. It needs a neutral pH, between 6.6 and 7.2, and a temperature between 70 and 85 degrees. In addition to food scraps, it should be fed prepared fish food.

The kuhli loach (Acanthophtalmus kuhlii) is another scavenger, like the catfish, recommended for any aquarium. Wormlike in appearance, the kuhli loach grows 3 or 4 inches in length. This fish also requires a neutral pH between 6.6 and 7.2, with a temperature between 70 and 85 degrees. It eats plant detritus and bottom scraps.

The Siamese fighting fish (Betta splendens) is a labyrinth fish that possesses a respiratory organ. This fish has long, wavy fins and comes in many color combinations, but red, green, and blue are preferred. If there is more than one male in a tank, they will fight with each other. The males build nests of bubbles in which eggs are deposited. Siamese fighting fish grow to about 2½ inches in length. They prefer temperatures between 76 and 85 degrees, with a pH of 6.8 to 7. They eat dried or live food.

Coral and marine plants form the habitat of these beautiful fish. The poor man's Moorish idol (*Heniochus acuminatus*) at right has a black-and-white striped body with yellow edging on its dorsal fin and tail. At left is a yellow tang (*Zebrasoma flavescens*). The shiny blue fish at top is a blue devil (*Abudefdul cyanea*). They all eat brine shrimp.

At left is a tomato clown fish (*Amphiprion frenatus*) with a red body and a white band around its head. It secretes a mucous that protects it from the deadly tentacles of some anemones. At right the skunk-striped clown fish (*Amphiprion akallopisos*) has a yellow body with a white trim illuminating its quill-like edging.

At upper left is a butterfly fish (*Chaetodon chrysurus*) marked with a black chevron pattern and an orange tail. Just below is a red-striped butterfly (*Chaetodon lunula*) that has a yellow body with black and white markings. In the center is a yellow-lined sweetlips (*Gaterin albovittatus*).

The Marine Tank

A saltwater tank is more difficult to maintain than a freshwater tank. Patience is the key to keeping the right chemical balance in sea water—there are no short cuts. But for the advanced fish keeper, the ability to reproduce a natural environment in a marine tank like those shown above and opposite is a source of great satisfaction.

Materials

Equipment needed for a saltwater tank is similar to that for a freshwater tank. But salt is a powerful destroyer of metal. The tank, lid, and equipment should be fabricated of glass or plastic. The size and the number of marine fish you will keep will determine the tank size. Special tools are used for measuring the density, temperature, pH level, salinity, and dissolved gases of the sea water.

The lo (*Lo vulpinus*) at top has a yellow body with a striped snout. Its spines are poisonous and can give a painful sting. The blue-and-black striped fish at center is a cleaner wrasse (*Labroides dimidiatus*). This fish buries itself at night or when it is alarmed. A sweetlips is near the bottom.

Positioning the Tank

Enough light must reach a saltwater tank to encourage the growth of algae. Algae constitute the main diet of marine fish and help eliminate toxic gases. In this case, the under-gravel filter is covered with 2 inches of dolomite chips, which help maintain the high alkalinity needed.

Synthetic Salt Water

Real sea water is as complex a solution as blood. Synthetic sea water used in aquariums is less complex, containing only what the fish need. Mixtures available for making sea water at home with tap water are easy to use by following package directions. As filters circulate the water, salt is combined in solution.

In a saltwater tank, the pH value of the water must be checked daily with a test kit. Most mixes are alkaline with a pH of 8 to 8.2, ideal for marine specimens. But if the alkali reserve becomes depleted, which can happen rapidly due to the buildup of waste products, changes in pH occur that are deadly for the fish.

In the salt water, the concentration of salt must be kept uniform. The sea water is checked once a week with a thermometer-hydrometer (photograph 10). This tool establishes the density of the salt water at a specific temperature.

A hydrometer is a glass tube weighted at one end, with a calibrated stem at the other. As the hydrometer floats, the stem above the water records the density of the water. The hydrometer should read 1022 to 1025 at 76 degrees. If the salinity registers below 1022, salt mix is added to the tank water, a pinch at a time. The salinity cannot be increased more than two points in a 24-hour period without endangering the fish. If the hydrometer recording is above 1025, a gallon or more of salt water is removed and replaced with tap water.

Marine Fishes

A good rule of thumb to use when selecting marine fish is to allow 3 inches of fish for each 5 gallons of water. This means six medium-sized fish can be kept in a 30-gallon tank. Marine specimens such as butterfly fish, damsels, clown fish, filefish, gobies, batfish, wrasses, and cardinals are colorful and compatible in a community tank. These come in small sizes, making it easy for the beginner to keep several of each. Some fish such as angels are territorial; they dominate areas of the tank and fight among themselves. So only one angelfish should be placed in a tank. Care must be taken in handling scorpion fish and lion fish; they possess toxic spines. Fish such as trunks and puffers excrete slime, which will foul a tank quickly. If sharks are added to a tank with smaller fish, the latter may be eaten.

For related projects, see "Ant Farms," "Birds and Bird Houses," "Insects," "Pet Habitats," and "Vivariums."

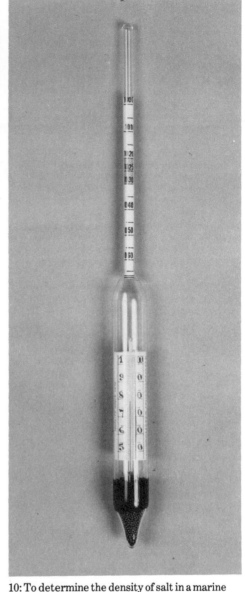

10: To determine the density of salt in a marine tank, put the rounded end of a combination hydrometer-thermometer in the water. As the hydrometer floats, the thermometer below the surface records the water temperature while the calibrated stem above the water measures the water density. The hydrometer should read 1022 to 1025 at 76 degrees Fahrenheit. If the density drops below 1022, raise the salinity by gradually adding pinches of salt to the outside filter box. But if the hydrometer reading rises above 1025, dilute the water by removing some salt water and adding tap water, a bit at a time, until the reading returns to the recommended density.

TYING FLIES

To Fool a Fish

For many, fishing is a business of huge nets and huge hauls. For others, it is a sport of power boats, strong tackle, and live bait. But for the fly fisherman, it is a solitary, quiet sport of wading boots, light tackle, and artificial flies. By the nature of his equipment, the fly fisherman is the least concerned with how many and how big are the fish that are caught, and is the most involved with the fish's environment.

The tackle of the fly fisherman is simple and responsive. The lighter the equipment is, the easier it is to present the fly, but the more difficult it is to land the fish. Presenting and landing are skills that can be learned only with years of fishing experience in different waters under varying conditions. But despite mastery of these skills, the ability to catch a fish ultimately depends on the fly itself—the bait made of bits of fur and feathers tied to a fishing hook.

The earliest artificial flies were simple imitations of water insects. Later, in the Victorian Age, beauty and style became dominant. The rivers were so rich with fish and the competition for them so limited that the flies' effectiveness was never truly tested. By the twentieth century, the fly tier was forced to design patterns that would have greater appeal to the fish. The emphasis shifted to less elaborate and more accurate patterns. Fish, it was observed, fed not only on water insects, imitated by the artificial fly, but also on the unhatched eggs of insects; so flies called nymphs were designed to duplicate them. Fish also fed on insects which floated on top of the water; so the dry fly was developed to take advantage of this feeding pattern. The Rat-Faced MacDougall, page 2648, is an example of a dry fly. Still popular were the more traditional wet flies; both the Royal Coachman, page 2650 and the TW Special, page 2645 are examples.

Given a sport demanding patience and sensitivity, it is not surprising that the angler often ties his own flies. Fly tying can be an imitative craft, following patterns that others have copied from nature. But it reaches its peak when the angler begins to experiment, to understand cause and effect, to know why a fish will react a certain way under particular conditions. The TW Special is one example of a fisherman's understanding and inspiration. When you begin to design your own patterns, you will need to understand why classic patterns do or don't work under certain circumstances, and that demands a study of fish and insect life which is the essence of fly fishing.

Ted Williams, best known as a professional baseball player with a particular affection for fast balls, is also a sportsman who devotes much attention to the Atlantic salmon. When the Marimechi River salmon season ends in the fall in New Brunswick, Canada, he heads for the bonefish and tarpon fishing off the Florida Keys. He is president of the Sports Advisory Board of Sears Roebuck and Company.

The fly box contains the fisherman's bait, with each fly representing a different insect or a different stage in a fly's development.

Opposite: Fly fishing involves casting to present an artificial fly at a precise location. A long, accurate cast will put the fly within sight of the fish. A slight wrist movement or the action of the current then animates the fly. The fly itself is tied to duplicate the shape and color of a natural food of the fish. The final stage, landing a hooked fish, requires a delicate feel for the strength of the fish, since too sudden a reel-in will break the light line.

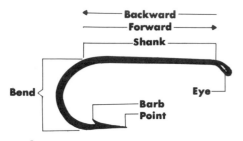

A
Figure A: The fishing line is connected to the eye of the hook. The shank extends from the eye to the spot where the hook begins to bend. Most fly-tying operations are done on the shank. When you select a hook, be sure its barb and point are sharp.

Sources for fly-tying materials
Angler's Roost
141 East 44th St.
New York, New York 10017

Dan Bailey's Flies and Tackle
209 West Park St.
Livingston, Montana 59047

Bodmer's Fly Shop
2400 Naegele Road
Colorado Springs, Colorado 80904

E. B. & H. A. Darbee
Rural Delivery
Livingston Manor, New York 12758

Fireside Angler, Inc.
P. O. Box 823
Melville, New York 11746

Herters, Inc.
Rural Route 1
Waseca, Minnesota 56093

E. Hille, Angler's Supply House Inc.
Williamsport, Pennsylvania 17701

Bud Lilly's Trout Shop
Box 387
West Yellowstone, Montana 59758

The Orvis Company, Inc.
Manchester, Vermont 05254

Rangeley Region Sports Shop
28 Main St.
Rangeley, Maine 04970

Sears, Roebuck and Company
Sporting Goods Department
(Check your telephone directory for local address.)

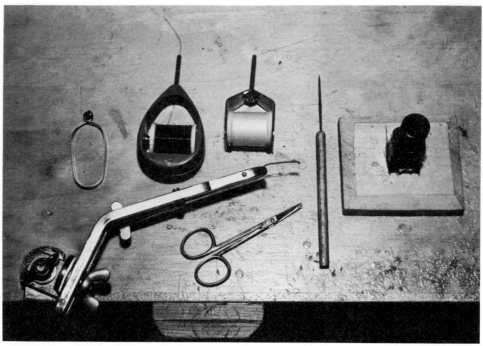

1: The fly tier's workbench, clockwise from the lower left, includes a vise, a hackle pliers, two bobbins, a dubbing needle, black lacquer, and scissors.

The Basic Workbench

The fly tier's tools (photograph 1) are simple and relatively inexpensive. The fly-tying vise clamps the hook tightly and holds it in place while the fly is tied. Traditional tiers often shun this modern convenience, using fingers instead, but for the novice the vise is a valuable aid. Hackle pliers are used for winding hackles (neck feathers) and flues (a fiber or barb of a feather) onto the hook. Bobbins house the tying thread and keep it taut when it is not being wrapped. A good bobbin, like either of those pictured, should be simple and without sharp edges.

Tying thread is used to tie fur and feathers on the hook. Silk was the preferred material for many years, but it has been supplanted by nylon which is less expensive, less subject to fraying, and stronger than silk. Nylon comes in a range of sizes and colors. For the projects that follow, black size-A thread is used. The scissors have straight, sharp blades; make sure to choose a pair with holes large enough for your fingers. The dubbing needle is used to apply black lacquer to the head of the fly. After the lacquer is applied, the needle is used to remove any lacquer clogging the eye of the hook. The lacquer also protects the knot that finishes the fly.

Fly Materials

An artificial fly is usually a combination of fur and feathers tied to a hook. The hooks come in a tremendous range of sizes, shapes, bends, shank lengths, eye styles, points, and finishes. Generally, light wire hooks are used for dry flies, heavier hooks for wet flies. The lower the number that is assigned to a hook, the longer it will be. A No. 8 hook is longer than a No. 10.

Feathers are used in flies to suggest insect parts. Among those commonly used are: hackles (neck feathers); tippets (feather tips); herls (a fiber or barb of a feather); and strands (hairlike feathers from the crest of a fowl). Projects that follow call for chicken hackles, peacock tail-feathers, pheasant crests, pheasant tail-feathers, and jungle-cock feathers.

Fur or animal hair is another common fly material. Mohair, squirrel hair, impala hair, and deer hair are used to make fly bodies and wings in the projects that follow.

Floss and tinsel are synthetic threads used for the tail end of the fly and for ribbings—windings around the body that imitate the flash, texture, and translucence of a water insect. Embroidery thread may be used for floss, and thin silver-colored household wire may be substituted for silver tinsel. A reputable supplier can help you select appropriate tools and materials; suppliers are listed at left.

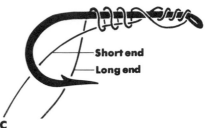

C
Figure C: To wrap the tying thread clockwise on the hook, first move forward three turns toward the eye, and then backward until an even base of thread covers the shank. The short end of thread is trimmed off; the long end, from the bobbin, is used to tie in all the materials added to the hook.

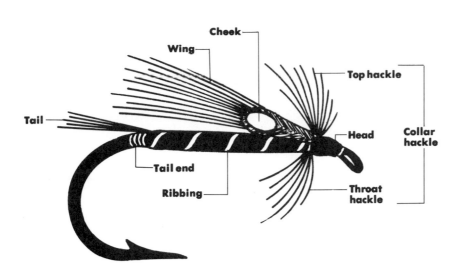

B
Figure B: Though there can be no single illustration of the anatomy of an artificial fly, since there are so many types, this drawing contains many of the elements present in the three flies described in the projects that follow. In the wet flies, the tail, tail end, body, body ribbing, throat, wings, cheeks, and head imitate the color, shape, and translucence of an aquatic fly. In the dry fly, the tail, body, and collar hackles are crucial in keeping the fly afloat.

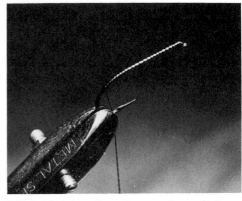

2: To begin tying a fly, put an even layer of tying thread on the shank of the hook. Flies that will have heavy wing or hackle feather dressings need an extra 15 to 20 wraps of tying thread just below the eye. The resulting bump will be your anchor.

Starting Up

Though there are a multitude of fly-tying styles, they all use three basic processes: starting up (winding a base of thread on the hook); tying in and tying off (securing other materials to the hook); and finishing (ending the tying with a series of knots to hold all the elements in place).

The first step, laying a base of thread on the hook, makes all the other tying procedures simpler and more secure.

To begin, check the hook for flaws such as an open eye or faulty point. Then secure the hook in a vise. Thread the bobbin with tying thread. Holding the bobbin in your right hand and the end of the thread taut in your left hand, wind the bobbin around the shaft of the hook three times (just below the eye, Figure C). Pull the short end (in your left hand) toward the point, and cover it with turns of tying thread until the shank is covered from the eye to a point even with the barb. Let the bobbin dangle to keep these windings taut on the hook. Trim the short end of the tying thread. Flies that will have elaborate wings and hackle tie-ins near the hook eye should have an extra 15 or 20 windings of tying thread just below the eye (photograph 2). This forms a ridge that will anchor the wings and hackles.

Tying In and Tying Off

The fur, feathers, tinsel, and floss that turn the hook into a fly are all secured to the hook with tying thread. Tying in is the term for securing one end of a material to the hook. Tying in is usually done with three tight wraps of tying thread. Place the material on the hook and make one turn of the thread, loosely securing the material. Adjust the material so it is properly positioned. Then tighten the first wrap and make two more tight turns. To keep the fly neat, snip off any excess from the tied-in end of material, close to the tying thread. Some fly parts need only be tied in with the three turns of tying thread. The opposite end is left free. In other cases the other end of the material being tied in must be tied to the hook; this is known as tying off. This is also accomplished with three tight wraps of tying thread. Again, excess material should be trimmed off with the scissors.

Tie-ins and tie-offs near the head often require more wraps. The additional thickness helps protect the fly and serves as a head. After any tie-in or tie-off, let the bobbin dangle. Its weight will keep the wraps tight on the hook.

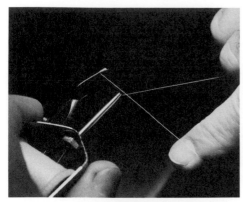

3: To start a whip-finish knot, use two fingers to make a triangle of the thread, with the end closest to the bobbin (left) on top.

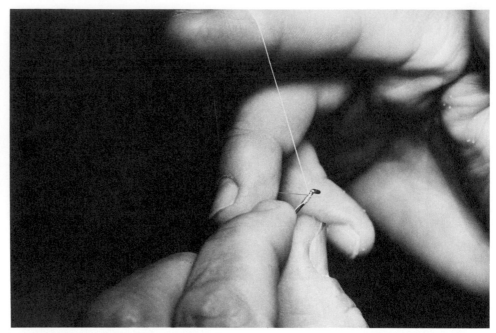

4: Next, twist the triangle over to put the hook end of the thread on top and slip it over the eye of the hook. This anchors the bobbin thread underneath the hook-end thread.

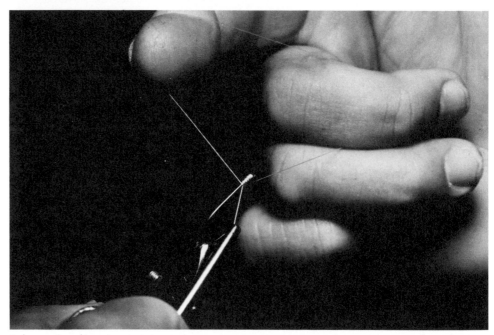

5: As you draw the triangle tight, the hook end of the thread will be anchored in place. Repeat this maneuver four times; then draw the bobbin back, tightening the last loop. Snip the tying thread close to this last loop, and you have a strong invisible knot.

Finishing-off

After all the materials have been tied in, apply a whip finish or invisible knot. This is the best fastening, both neat and secure, but it is a maneuver you should practice on a bare hook.

As shown in photograph 3, you start a whip-finish knot by forming a triangle with the thread near the hook and near the bobbin, keeping the bobbin-end thread on top. As you bring the triangle over the hook, you twist it once so the hook-end thread is on top, and is the thread that loops the hook (photograph 4). When the threads are tightened, the hook end of the thread anchors the bobbin end (photograph 5). Repeat this maneuver four times to make a secure whip-finish knot.

Materials
Hook: No. 10
Head: Black lacquer
Tail: Golden-pheasant crest
Tail end: Silver tinsel and yellow floss
Body: Black mohair
Ribbing: Silver tinsel
Throat: Black hackle
Wings: Dyed red impala hair and natural squirrel fur
Cheeks: Artificial jungle-cock feathers

7: Begin the TW Special with wraps of silver tinsel and yellow floss. Trim the floss close to the tying thread, but leave the silver tinsel, used for the tip, uncut. It dangles out of the way and will be used later as ribbing over a mohair body.

6: Materials used to make the TW Special are, clockwise from the top; squirrel fur, jungle-cock feathers, black mohair, silver tinsel, yellow floss, red impala hair, golden-pheasant crest feathers, and black hackle feathers. The completed TW Special is at the bottom of the photograph.

Outdoor Activities
The TW special $ ⧗ 👪 🦞

The TW Special was designed especially for fishing for Atlantic salmon. It is a wet fly (one that sinks in water), imitating insect life in the river. It is made of squirrel fur, red impala hair, mohair, tinsel, floss, and feathers (photograph 6). To begin, set a No. 10 hook in the tying vise. Wrap the tying thread on the hook shank (page 2643), with an extra 15 or 20 turns placed just below the eye to form the head. The resulting bump will eventually be used as an anchor when you tie in the wings.

To form the tail end of the fly (Figure B, page 2643), place the end of the silver-tinsel thread on the under side of the shank opposite the point, and tie it in with three wraps of tying thread. Snip off the short end of the tinsel close to the tying thread. With the tying-thread bobbin hanging out of the way, wrap the tinsel toward the hook end, making eight tight turns; then make eight tight forward turns toward the eye so the tinsel ends where it began. Tie off the tinsel with tying thread but do not trim it; it will be used later as body ribbing. Next, tie in the bright yellow floss with three wraps of tying thread. Put three backward wraps of floss over the tinsel tip, come forward with three more wraps, and tie off the floss. Trim both ends of floss close to the tying thread (photograph 7).

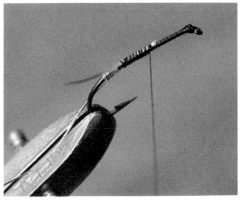

8: Make the tail with 20 strands of golden-pheasant crest, tying it in just in front of the yellow floss, halfway between the point and the eye. Tail ends extend beyond the curve of the hook. Three wraps of tying thread will tie it off.

To simulate a tail, secure 20 strands of golden-pheasant crest with three wraps of tying thread directly in front of the floss. The tip of the feather should extend beyond the bend of the hook, while the butt of the feather should be secured to the shank with tying thread, halfway between the point and the eye (photograph 8). Tie off with three turns of thread and trim the excess butt end of the feather.

Start the mohair body directly in front of the tail tie-off. With three wraps of tying thread, secure a long 1-to-2-foot length of mohair to the hook. Clamp the hackle pliers to the other end of the mohair, and rotate the pliers so the strands of mohair twist. Wrap the mohair back to the yellow floss, then forward to the tying thread.

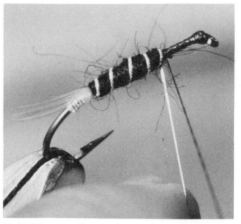

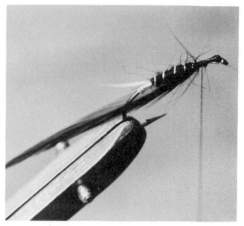

9: To make the body, tie in strands of mohair and wrap them back and forth, twisting with the hackle pliers as you wrap. The body has a slight taper, achieved with several extra turns put on near the center of the body section.

10: Holding the silver tinsel in your fingers, wrap it around the mohair, spacing it evenly, to make the body ribbing. Tie off the ribbing just in front of the body. This sparkle of silver tinsel is an important quality in a wet fly.

11: Start the collar by tying the butt end of a long black hackle feather to the hook, just behind the head. Hackle most often comes from a cock or hen chicken. In water, the throat section of a collar will simulate the kick of an insect's legs.

12: Holding the tip end of the hackle feather with a hackle pliers, wrap the feather around the hook five times to create the collar.

Wrap back and forth several times more, making three or four extra wraps in the center of the body to achieve the taper shown in photograph 9. Tie off the mohair body where you tied it in.

To make the body ribbing, wrap the silver tinsel forward in five evenly spaced turns over the mohair body (photograph 10). Tie it off with tying thread. Trim the excess mohair and tinsel.

Tie in the butt end of a long section of black hackle feather near the eye of the hook so the tips of the hackle extend well beyond the bend of the hook (photograph 11). Clamp the tip end of the hackle with a hackle pliers and wrap it five times around the hook, being careful not to crowd the head (photograph 12). Tie off this collar and trim away all except those hackle strands which flow down and toward the point of the hook (photograph 13). The remaining strands form the throat.

13: Trim off the hackle until you have left only those strands which flow down perpendicular to the shank and back toward the hook's point. The remaining black hackle constitutes the throat of the TW Special wet fly.

14: After you have tied 10 to 20 strands of red impala to the hook, tie in 30 to 50 strands of squirrel fur. They should extend to the bend of the hook, but not cover the tail. Use ten wraps to secure the section of squirrel fur.

15: Line the artificial jungle-cock feathers on the sides of the head so that the feather markings are behind the head. These feathers, called the cheeks, are considered a special flourish on a fly; some fly tiers leave them off.

16: The TW Special is completed with a whip finish of the tying thread (page 2644) and a black lacquer head. Apply the lacquer carefully with a dubbing needle so you do not clog the hook eye.

The wings will be formed with red impala hair and squirrel fur. Start by placing 10 to 20 strands of red impala on top of the collar tie-off. Tie in the impala so the tips are even with the bend of the hook. It is a good idea to wet the impala hair so you can judge how far back it will lie when the fly is in the water. On top of the impala, tie in a small bunch of squirrel fur (30 to 50 strands) with ten turns of tying thread (photograph 14). Trim off all the hair in front of the tying thread.

Finally, two artificial jungle-cock feathers are placed on the sides of the head, butt end forward, so that the circular pattern of the feathers falls slightly behind the head (photograph 15). Tie these in with five turns of thread, and snip off the feathers in front of the tying thread. Whip-finish the tying thread to complete the fly (page 2644). Coat the head with black lacquer, being careful not to clog the hook eye (photograph 16). The head is an important element of a wet fly.

Materials

Hook: No. 4 Dry Fly
Head color: Black
Tail: Hairs from the neck of a deer
Body: Cream-colored deer body-hair
Collar: Brown hackle tippet and ginger hackle tippet

17: The finished Rat-Faced MacDougall rests on a bed of brown hackle. To the left is Rock Plymouth hen hackle-tippet and to the right is cream-colored deer body-hair, ginger hackle, and deer neck-hair.

18: To start the Rat-Faced MacDougall, make a tail of deer neck-hair. Tie it to the shank, opposite the point, with three sets of tying-thread wraps. This keeps the tail parallel to the shank, preventing the rear of the hook from sinking.

19: After you tie in a section of deer body-hair and pull the thread tight enough so the hair flares, trim excess hair behind the tie-in wrap.

Outdoor Activities
The Rat-Faced MacDougall

Dry flies are designed to float on top of the water. Their fur and feathers are usually light and sometimes hollow; perhaps the most important floating ingredient is hackle. Dry flies are often used in low, warm water where fish are likely to be feeding on floating insects. The dry fly shown left and opposite is known as a Rat-Faced MacDougall. It was originally developed for trout fishing, but now it is most widely used for salmon fishing. It is made of deer hair and feathers (photograph 17). To begin, wrap an even base of tying thread on the shank of a No. 4 dry-fly hook (page 2643). Since there are no elaborate tie-ins to be made near the head, there is no need to build up a hump as in the TW Special (page 2645) and the Royal Coachman (page 2650).

To make the tail, take a small clump of the deer neck-hair (approximately 20 strands) and rest it on top of the shank so that it extends 1 inch beyond the curve of the hook. Use three wraps of tying thread to secure the hair to the shank even with the hook point. To keep the tail flat on the hook, make two additional sets of three wraps behind the first tie-in, with a small interval between sets (photograph 18). Trim excess hair in front of the tying thread.

The Floating Body

The body is formed by tying on bunches of deer body-hair so bristly cut ends flare up; smoother tip ends are trimmed off. Cut a small bunch of cream-colored deer body-hair (approximately 40 strands). With the natural tips held in your fingers, let about ½ inch of hair extend in front of the tying thread at the front of the tail. Put one turn of tying thread around the deer hair, and with the thread kept just tight enough to hold the hair, distribute the strands evenly around the hook shank. Then pull the wrap of tying thread very tight, until the hair in front of it flares up. With the tying thread kept taut, trim the hair behind the thread (photograph 19). To secure this first section of flared deer hair, zigzag two or three turns of tying thread through it. Brush this first section of deer body-hair back with your fingers so you can take the tying thread through the hair and out onto the hook shank, as close to the base of the hair as possible.

Tie the next section of deer body-hair as close to the front of the first as possible, with ½ inch of cut ends in front of the tying thread. Again distribute the hair evenly, tighten the tying thread, trim excess hair, zigzag the thread through the area where the two sections meet, and move the tying thread through the brushed-back deer hair. Continue to add sections, keeping them as close together as possible. You should be able to tie on about seven sections and still have enough room behind the hook eye for wings and collar hackle (photograph 20). After you complete the final section, take the thread forward onto the hook shank and secure it with a whip finish (page 2644). Cut off the tying thread.

Remove the hook from the vise, and trim the deer body-hair with a scissors (photograph 21). Trim a little at a time, cutting away from the tail and shaping the body into an elongated oval, tapering it toward the rear. The bottom side of the body is trimmed shorter and flatter than the top to preserve the bite of the hook.

The Wings and Collar

After you have shaped the body contour, put the hook back in the vise and wrap on the tying thread again (page 2643). The securing wraps should be just in front of the whip-finish knot. For the wings, use two small tippets of Rock-Plymouth-hen hackle. With the tips extending beyond the hook eye, tie them to the top of the shank with three tight turns of thread. Leave a small space between the body and wings for two collar hackles. To get the wing to form an upright V-shape, first raise the wings and put two wraps of tying thread in front of them (photograph 22). Around one of the wings, make a series of loops with the tying thread, going from front right to rear left and rear right to front left, putting pressure on the tippet as you loop rearward to force it to stand up. Repeat this operation with the other wing. Make three wraps of tying thread behind the wings; then cut off the excess tippet material behind the tying thread.

20: Tie on as many sections of deer hair as you can, leaving just enough room next to the hook eye for the wings and collar hackle. Seven sections were used in this fly.

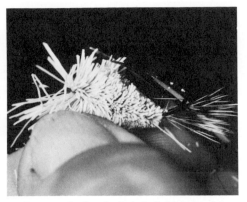

21: To taper the deer body-hair, hold the hook in your fingers and trim with a scissors, cutting away from the tail and being careful not to snip it off accidentally.

22: To raise the wings into a V shape, loop the thread around each, making sure the thread is pulled very tight. Otherwise the wings might be pulled out of line when the hackles are tied on.

23: The hackle collar is the crucial element of a dry fly. To make it, use the hackle pliers to twist each feather six times around the shank—three turns behind the wings and three in front. That will keep the head of the fly afloat.

The Rat-Faced MacDougall is a dry fly meant to imitate a floating insect. Dry flies are of relatively recent origin; size and shape are much more important to their success than color.

The last element, the collar, is the most important part of an effective dry fly (Figure B, page 2643). For this, use equal lengths of one ginger hackle and one brown hackle tippet. Tie them in just beyond the two wings so their tips extend over the hook eye. Grasp one of the hackles with the hackle pliers and make three tight turns behind the wings, working forward, then three tight turns in front of the wings (photograph 23). Tie off the hackle with three turns of tying thread, and trim the excess hackle tip. Repeat the procedure with the second hackle. After trimming the second hackle tip, secure the fly with a whip finish (page 2644). Cut off the tying thread and remove the fly from the vise. Paint the head with black lacquer, being careful not to clog the hook eye. The head of a dry fly is less pronounced than that of a wet fly.

Materials

Hook: No. 6 Wet Fly

Head: Black lacquer

Tail end: Silver tinsel thread and golden-pheasant tippet

Butt: 6 peacock herls taken from just below the eye of the feather

Body: Red floss

Wings: Natural white impala

Collar: Brown hackle

24: The materials of the Royal Coachman, clockwise from the upper left, are white impala hair, peacock herl, brown hackle, red floss, silver tinsel, and golden-pheasant tippet. At the bottom is the finished Royal Coachman.

Outdoor Activities
The Royal Coachman

Within a 500-year tradition of tying artificial flies which resemble the real thing, there have been aberrations—fly patterns without natural precedents. The Royal Coachman, believed to have caught more fish than any other fly pattern, is the prime example of a fly inspired solely by the imagination. Reputedly, it was devised by Queen Victoria's coachman for use in trout fishing. It has since evolved into a multipurpose fly used to catch salmon, panfish, bass, steelhead, and shad.

To start a Coachman, wrap a No. 6 hook with a layer of tying thread, putting an extra 15 to 20 wraps around the base of the eye for anchoring the wing and collar sections (page 2643). Place a length of silver tinsel on the shank, even with the hook's point, and secure it with three wraps of tying thread. Make five backward wraps with the tinsel, then five forward wraps, and tie off with three turns of tying thread. Trim excess tinsel.

For the tail, cut a small clump of golden-pheasant tippet (10 to 20 strands) and tie it in just ahead of the tinsel. The black tips should extend 1 inch beyond the hook bend (photograph 25). Trim excess tippet in front of the thread.

The Coachman Body

The body of the Coachman consists of a long section of red floss with clusters of peacock herl at either end. Tie in three peacock herls by their tips just in front of the tail. Grasp the butts of the peacock herl in one hand and an equal length of tying thread in the other and gently twist them together (photograph 26). Being careful not to break the delicate peacock herl, wrap the twisted herl and thread forward ten times in a close cluster. Untwist excess herl and tie off with three turns of tying thread. Trim off the excess herl (photograph 27).

Wrap the tying thread forward on the shank until it covers two-thirds of the distance between the point and the eye. At this spot on the shank, tie in the red floss with three turns of thread. Wrap the floss a few turns back toward the peacock cluster. Wrap the tying thread back four turns over the red floss to anchor it; then move the tying thread forward four turns to its original position (photograph 28). This will secure the body floss. Wrap the floss all the way back to the peacock cluster, then forward to the starting point, then back and forth twice more. Tie off the red floss with three turns of tying thread, and snip off the remaining floss. Tie in three more peacock herls just in front of the red floss. Using the same twist and turn procedure, duplicate the rear herl cluster (photograph 29). Trim off excess herl.

To make the wings, take a cluster of white impala hair (20 to 30 strands) and tie it in just in front of the second peacock cluster, using ten turns of tying thread. The tips of the impala should extend to the hook bend, but should not obscure the golden-pheasant tail (photograph 30). Trim excess impala in front of the tying thread.

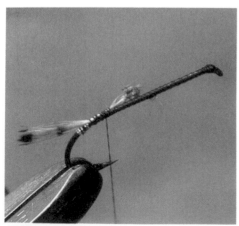

25: When you tie in the golden-pheasant tippet to make the tail, position the black tips so they are even and straight.

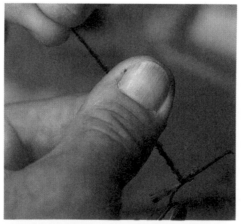

26: Holding the tying thread and peacock herl as shown, one in each hand, twist them together very gently; the herl may break under pressure.

27: Tie off the peacock herl with three wraps of tying thread. Trim away the excess herl not caught by the tying thread.

28: To secure the red body floss, tie it on two-thirds of the distance between the point and the eye, using four backward and four forward wraps.

29: Make a front cluster of peacock herl that duplicates the butt section. Be careful not to crowd the head of the fly.

30: To make the wings, tie on white impala hair with ten wraps of tying thread. Be sure the wings will not hide the tail when the fly is in the water.

31: Clamp the brown hackle in the hackle pliers and wrap it around the shank five times to make the collar. Unlike dry flies, wet flies do not require heavy hackle collars.

The Royal Coachman is probably the most popular and successful dry-fly pattern ever devised. Since it bears no resemblance to any insect, its success is perplexing to fly tiers, who carefully study and imitate life on and in the water.

Further fly reading
Art Flick's Master Fly-Tying Guide by Art Flick, Ed Koch, Lefty Kreh, Ted Niemeyer, Carl Richards, Ernest Schwiebert, Helen Shaw, Doug Swisher, Dave Whitlock. Crown Publishers, Inc., New York, N.Y.

The Art of Tying the Wet Fly & Fishing the Flymph by James E. Leisenring and Vernon S. Hidy. Crown Publishers, Inc., New York, N.Y.

Atlantic Salmon Flies & Fishing by Joseph D. Bates, Jr. Stackpole Books, Harrisburg, Pennsylvania.

Creative Fly Tying and Fly Fishing by Rex Gerlach. Winchester Press, New York, N.Y.

A Modern Dry-Fly Code by Vincent C. Marinaro. Crown Publishers, Inc., New York, N.Y.

The Practical Fly Fisherman by A. J. McClane. Prentice-Hall, Inc., Englewood, N.J.

To make the collar, tie in the butt end of a brown hackle feather in front of the impala hair. Using the hackle pliers, make five close wraps of hackle on the shaft (photograph 31). Tie off the hackle with five turns of thread; then make a whip-finish knot (page 2644). Snip off excess hackle and tying thread.

Remove the hook from the vise and paint the head with black lacquer, using a dubbing needle. Avoid clogging the hook eye with lacquer.

For related projects, see "Beachcombing," "Fur Recycling," "Insects," "Rope Knotting," "Sashimi and Sushi," and "Tropical Fish."

UPHOLSTERY
A High Recovery Rate

That old upholstered chair or sofa in an attic or second-hand store may have popped a few springs and lost some stuffing. But beneath its ragged appearance you might find a well made piece of furniture that can be restored and reupholstered for many more years of use.

Few crafts have been more concerned with providing creature comfort through the years than upholstery. Although the practice of padding furniture didn't come into widespread use until the seventeenth century, the possibility of achieving softer seating with dried grass was tried by the ancient Egyptians.

No matter how attractive a piece of furniture may look, the crucial test is in the sitting. Often, an uncomfortable chair or couch is one whose insides have given out: the springs have sprung or the padding has become lumpy. Restoring its former comfort can be accomplished with only a few tools and new materials. However, upholstery does require slow, patient, and careful workmanship. Some projects may take only a few hours, but others will require complete disassembly and refinishing, with work being done in several stages over many days.

Most projects involve the reupholstery of previously upholstered furniture, and in such cases it is important to remove the old materials carefully and to observe how they were assembled. Often, the old fabrics can be used as patterns for the new. It is a good idea to take notes, make sketches, even take photographs of each layer of construction. This will give you an accurate working guide for installing replacement materials.

Old furniture bears the scars of earlier upholstery work; sometimes the wood has been badly splintered by overtacking. You can avoid further wood stress by using new tacks a little smaller than would ordinarily be used on new work.

Before you begin a project, choose a clean and well lighted work area, if possible one away from household traffic so you can leave the work-in-progress there until it is finished. As you remove tacks and staples, discard them; they are not worth trying to salvage. Do the same with any pieces of old cambric and muslin that you do not need as patterns. Genuine horsehair stuffing, however, should be saved. It is one of the best padding materials available and is quite expensive. It can be restored to usefulness by washing it in warm, soapy water, picking apart any matted areas, and drying it atop a window screen or other airy surface.

Buying Used Furniture
Second-hand shops and estate auctions are places to buy used furniture in need of reupholstering. Since you will discard all of the covering material and most of the stuffing, choose a piece for its lines and the condition of its frame. If the frame is damaged, it will have to be taken apart, reglued, and refinished before the piece is reupholstered. Such work is tedious and worth the effort only if the piece is quite valuable or if you already own it.

 Because upholstery fabric takes a certain amount of abuse and because it is the dominant decorative feature, choose it with care. Know its fiber content. If you are unsure of its durability, ask. Heavy fabrics hold tacks well, hide imperfections in stuffing, and tend to look rich. But they are hard to handle at corners and where they overlap. Medium weights such as corduroy, linen, sailcloth, satin, and damask are easier to use and generally better for beginners. Lightweight fabrics tend to pull away from tacks and should be avoided. If you select a patterned fabric, consider its scale in relation to the size of the piece of furniture being covered and the room in which it will be used.

Dan Goshern (left) learned the basics of upholstery at his father's shop in Cincinnati, Ohio. After attending the University of Cincinnati, he opened his own upholstery shop, doing work ranging from restoring antiques to making stuffed animals for an amusement park. His home is in Sag Harbor, Long Island. Dan's work appears on pages 2654 through 2658.

At an early age, Pat Kern (right) decided to find a trade to be his life's work. After an apprenticeship at a custom upholstery shop in Indiana, he decided he liked the challenge involved in the craft of upholstery. He has long operated his own shop in the historic whaling village of Sag Harbor, Long Island, where his work has ranged from museum antiques, to modern sculpture, to restoring furnishings of the former summer White House of President Kennedy at Hyannis Port, Mass. Pat reupholstered the chair on page 2659.

As a look into a corner of an upholsterer's workroom indicates, this is a craft that calls for more skill than equipment. At center, from bottom to top, are mallet and chisel, wire cutters, tack hammer, glue, tack puller, scissors, jute webbing, burlap, and cotton padding. A box of tacks is with the stripped-down frame at right, upholstery fabrics in front of the finished project at left. One essential tool not in the photograph is the webbing stretcher (page 2655).

Cutting the fabric

If you are taking direct measurements rather than using the old fabric as a pattern, measure the width of each section of the chair first. Most upholstery fabrics come in 54-inch widths. If you use a patterned fabric, particularly one with large, bold motifs, consider how you will place and match these motifs before you cut the fabric. Some upholsterers prefer to cover an entire chair with muslin before adding upholstery fabric; mistakes made in cutting muslin are far less costly to correct than with fabric.

An upholstered stool, 10 inches high, 10 inches wide, and 17 inches long, adds a bright note to the room decor and provides a comfortable extra seat near the fireplace. Such a project provides a simple introduction to the craft of upholstering.

Furniture and Refinishing
A cushioned bench

The most ordinary stool (or even a wooden box) can be turned into a useful and comfortable piece of furniture for extra seating with the addition of an upholstered top. If the legs are scarred, hide them with a skirt. To make the stool shown above I used a frame of 1-by-4-inch pine, 10 inches wide and 17 inches long, to which 10-inch legs of 2-by-2-inch pine were nailed. If you are using an old stool, make sure the rails are sound enough to hold tacks.

Tools needed for this project are: a sharp knife; scissors; a tack puller; an upholster's magnetized tack hammer; and a webbing stretcher. Materials used include: 2½ yards of jute webbing, 3½ inches wide; several boxes of No. 6 and No. 2 upholstery tacks; and a 3-inch-thick piece of foam rubber ½ inch longer and ½ inch wider than the frame (photograph 1). Upholstery supply stores and some hardware stores carry these or similar items. In addition you will need ½ yard of 36-inch-wide upholstery fabric and muslin, and 1½ yards of finished welting. If you make your own welting you will need 1 or 1¼ yards of fabric.

Start by placing the stool on a flat work surface. Correct any wobbling by rasping or sanding the long leg.

1: Tools and materials used to upholster a stool include (clockwise from right): a block of foam rubber and sharp knife, webbing stretcher, magnetized tack hammer, tack-pulling tool, scissors, upholstery tacks, jute webbing, and a strip of foam rubber (cut from larger piece) for side padding. Also needed are upholstery fabric and welting.

A
Figure A: A webbing stretcher is an indispensable tool for insuring uniform tautness in the jute webbing of upholstered furniture. The untoothed end of the tool, here covered with ridged rubber to forestall slipping, is held against the outside of the seat frame. A length of webbing, tacked at the opposite end, is pulled across the frame and caught on the sharp teeth of the stretcher as it is held at about a 30-degree angle up from the frame. As downward pressure is applied on the stretcher, the webbing is stretched drumhead-tight.

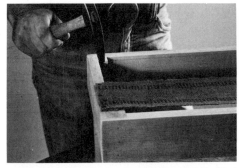

2: Fold 1 inch of jute webbing under itself and hold the fold flush against one end of the stool frame. Do not cut the strip loose from the roll.

3: Drive five No. 6 tacks through the folded end of webbing into the end rail. Follow a staggered pattern, but keep tacks ⅜ inch in from the edges.

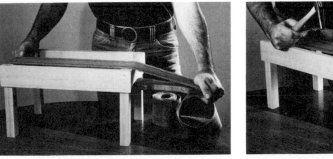

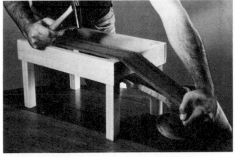

4: The webbing stretcher (right) serves as a lever to pull the webbing very tightly across the frame. The pointed teeth of the stretcher (Figure A) grip the webbing; the opposite end is wedged against the end rail.

5: Brace the frame against yourself while you exert downward pressure on the stretcher. A magnetized tack hammer permits you to drive tacks with one hand. Hammer four No. 6 tacks in a straight row, ⅜ inch from the outside.

6: Cut off the webbing, leaving ½ inch extra to be doubled back. Fold this excess back over the frame and tack it down with three more tacks, using a staggered pattern (⅜ inch from the inside of the rail) to avoid hitting the tacks beneath.

Mark guidelines on the frame, the width of the webbing strips, so they will be evenly spaced with two running lengthwise and one crosswise. Even, close spacing of the webbing distributes weight and forestalls sagging. (While a single cross strip is adequate for this simple project, in chairs or sofas it is best to use as many webbing strips as you can fit in, generally spacing them about an inch apart.)

Lay the free end of webbing within the marked guidelines of one of the shorter sides of the stool, folding 1 inch of webbing under itself (photograph 2). Tack the webbing to the frame with five to seven tacks, staggering the tacks rather than putting them in a straight line to avoid splitting the wood or tearing the webbing (photograph 3). Place the other end of the webbing with corresponding guidelines, and use a webbing stretcher to pull the webbing taut across the frame (photograph 4 and Figure A). Tack the single layer of webbing down with four tacks in a straight row, ⅜ inch from the outside of the rail (photograph 5). Cut the webbing with a

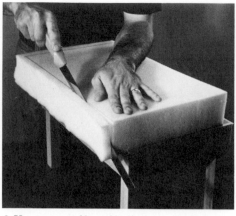

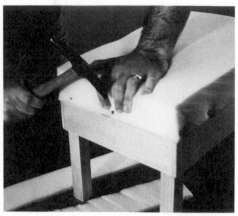

7: Using the same stretching and tacking techniques, add a lengthwise band parallel with the first, starting it at the opposite end. Weave a crosswise band into place; center and tack it.

8: Use a serrated bread knife to saw the foam block to exactly the size of the bench frame. Two ¼-inch-thick slices trimmed from one side and two from one end can be used later for side padding.)

9: When the foam block has been trimmed to match the size of the stool frame, tack the foam to the frame. Using No. 6 tacks, catch the lower edge of the foam and tack into the top of the frame.

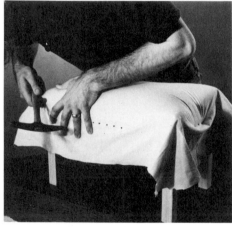

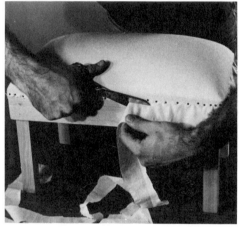

10: Cover the foam with a piece of muslin large enough to hide the side panels. Stay-tack it at the center of one of the long sides, using two or three No. 2 tacks ½ inch below the frame top to hold the muslin. Brace the tacked side against yourself, pull the muslin taut to the opposite side, and stay-tack it there. Then stay-tack the two ends the same way before you begin extending the rows of tacks toward the corners.

11: After you have driven tacks at 1-inch intervals all around the stool rail, the muslin should be taut and smooth as shown. Use scissors to trim off the surplus muslin about ¼ inch below the tacks.

12: The decorative upholstery fabric covers the muslin. Tack it in place just as you did the muslin, placing the tacks just below the first row. Trim the fabric about an inch below the tacks.

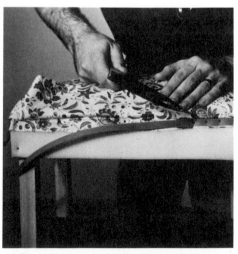

13: Stretch a strip of welt (cord encased in upholstery fabric) along one side of the seat frame. Tack it to the frame just below the seam that holds the cord in place. Continue tacking until the welt is in place on all four sides, making an invisible joint where the ends meet, as shown in Figure B.

14: Cover the top edge of the side panel with ½-inch tacking strips of cardboard, pressed snugly against the welt. The side fabric will be dropped down over the cardboard strip that holds it, concealing the tacks. The bottom edge will then be tacked to the inside of the seat frame.

scissors, allowing ½ inch extra to fold back. Turn the end back on itself and drive three more tacks, staggering them so you do not hit those below (photograph 6). Using the same technique but starting at the opposite end, tack a parallel band of webbing to the frame with the same degree of tautness. You can flatten the webbing folds, if they do not lie flat, by tapping them down with any hammer that is not magnetized. Attach a third webbing strip crosswise, weaving it under one lengthwise band and over the other. This completes the stool webbing (photograph 7).

Lay the foam-rubber block on a flat surface, and place the inverted stool on top of it so two adjacent sides line up with sides of the foam. With a pencil trace the outer edges of the frame where the foam projects. Turn the stool right side up, place the foam on top of it, and cut the foam to size with a sharp knife (photograph 8). If you do not trim all of the excess off at once but slice it in two ¼-inch-thick strips lengthwise and two ¼-inch-thick strips crosswise, you can use these thin strips as side padding later. The foam rectangle that finally remains should be cut along the traced pencil lines. Place the foam on the stool and tack it to the frame, catching the lower edges of the foam at 4-inch intervals (photograph 9).

Cut a rectangle of muslin large enough to cover the foam and the rails of the stool, in this case 21 by 23 inches. Stay-tack the muslin with three or four tacks near the middle of one side of the frame, pull the muslin taut, and stay-tack it the same way on the other side. Do the same at the ends. (When you stay-tack, you don't drive the tacks all the way in; this lets you lift them easily to make corrections.) Then drive additional tacks at 1-inch intervals on all sides, tacking from the centers of the rails toward the corners (photograph 10). This row of tacks should be within ½ inch of the top of the rails. As you tack, keep smoothing and stretching the muslin so it is held evenly by the tacks. If lumps or bulges appear in the crown (the high center of the foam cushion) pull out several tacks with the tack remover and reset them. Finally, drive all tacks fully into place. At the corners, fold the muslin over itself and tack it flat against the frame. Trim the muslin ¼ inch below the tack heads (photograph 11).

Covering
Cut a rectangle of upholstery fabric the same size as you originally cut the muslin, and tack it to the sides of the frame over the muslin in the same way (photograph 12). Place the row of tacks just below those holding the muslin. Trim the upholstery fabric an inch below the tacks.

Use welt—cord encased in 1½-inch-wide bias strips of upholstery fabric and stitched in place—to finish the edge of the padded top. (Welt is sometimes called piping.) Prepare enough welt to reach completely around the stool (Figure B). Ready-made welt can be purchased, if you prefer. Tack the welt in place, using the part just below the cord. The tacks will not show (photograph 13).

Side Panels
The strips of foam trimmed off the top block, approximately ¼ inch thick, will now be used to pad the outside of the rails. Cut them to the same width and slightly longer than these rails. Tack each strip to the rail, one tack to a corner. Position each strip so the excess foam can be bent around a corner of the stool to pad the sharp edge. Tack the foam in place at 4-inch intervals, top and bottom.

Cut a strip of covering material, long enough to wrap around the frame over the foam and deep enough to cover the side panels with an inch to spare.

Position the upholstery strip, reverse side up, across one side of the seat top, with a ½-inch allowance extending below the welt. Tack a narrow strip of cardboard over this allowance, pushing it tight against the bottom of the welt as you tack (photograph 14). Drop the upholstery strip down from time to time to make sure this blind tacking is as snug as it should be. With the upholstery strip reverse side up, continue blind tacking with cardboard strips around all four sides. When the last tack is in place, drop the fabric down over the side padding, pull it smooth over the bottom of the frame, and tack it to the inside of the frame. Again, start at the middle of each rail and work toward the corners.

Finish the stool by hand sewing the open corner of the side strip of upholstery fabric. If you add glides to the legs of the stool, those made of plastic do less damage to rugs than metal.

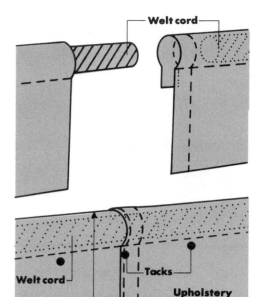

B
Figure B: To make an almost invisible welt joint, snip open the seams of both ends of the welt where they meet. Fold back the covering material of one of the ends and cut the cord about ¼ inch shorter than the cover. Fold back the fabric on the other end so the cord projects that amount. Fit the two cords together and fold the material of the cut end over the uncut end so they join smoothly. Tack the joined welt to the frame.

15: The folded-back seat materials reveal jute webbing (still tacked to the frame), burlap, horsehair padding, muslin, and leather, the latter originally set with closely spaced brass tacks.

Before: Even a leather-seated English side chair from the early nineteenth century looks distressed when the seat pad is worn and packed flat.

After: Identical seat construction but new materials (excepting only the washed and fluffed horsehair padding) restores both elegance and comfort.

Furniture and Refinishing
A padded chair seat

Years of use inevitably compress the padded seats of side chairs to a point where they are no longer comfortable. Reupholstering is the cure. Since only the seat pad is involved, in most cases this is a rather simple undertaking.

However, there are many ways to pad a side chair. Be careful, as you dismantle a chair, to observe how the work was done originally. The method described here was devised to match the original upholstery removed from the chair pictured above.

In photograph 15, the covering materials of the chair have been folded back to show the layers of padding you may encounter in this type of seat. Over a webbing tacked to this frame are layers of burlap, horsehair, muslin, and leather.

In this case I used identical new materials to restore the chair to its original condition. For a small side chair, you will need: suitable upholstery material (in this case, leather); muslin; burlap; padding (here, horsehair); and the tools shown on page 2655. After removing the old webbing and tacks, attach the new webbing with No. 6 upholstery tacks, pulled taut with a webbing stretcher (page 2655). If the wood has been splintered, use a smaller tack. Then new webbing should be interwoven with two crosswise and two lengthwise strips. Next, tack a covering of burlap over the webbing, using No. 2 tacks.

If the original stuffing material was horsehair, wash it, fluff it up, and dry it; then spread it over the burlap covering. Alternatively, new felted cotton or rubberized hair can be used. Rubberized hair comes in 24-inch rolls of various thicknesses. To contain the stuffing, measure and cut a piece of muslin large enough to overlap the sides by 2 inches. Tack the muslin in place to the frame, using No. 2 tacks and working from the middle of the sides into the corners. Cut away the excess muslin. If the final covering is to be a material other than leather, add a layer of felted cotton atop the muslin before tacking on the outer covering. Here, a dyed leather 1/32 inch thick was used, cut large enough to cover the seat with a ½-inch hem allowance all around. Turning the hem allowance under as I proceeded, I lightly stay-tacked the leather at the centers of the four sides, then tacked down the rest of the four sides, working toward the corners and pulling the material taut and smooth with my free hand as I drove the tacks with the other. The decorative brass-headed tacks abut around the edge of the seat. Tack heads will cut through leather if hammered too hard.

Furniture and Refinishing
A stuffed easy chair

$ 🗓️30 🧍 ⚗️

Stuffed furniture (sometimes called overstuffed) includes easy chairs, sofas, chaise longues, and the like. The traditional construction involves coil springs in the seat, and sometimes the back and arms, upholstered with layers of such materials as burlap, muslin, cotton, horsehair, foam, and covering fabric. The tools needed are those listed on page 2654. In addition, you need: jute cord and nylon tufting twine; a curved upholstery needle; a length of fox edging or roll edging for the front edge of the seat (page 2662); and several sizes of tacks.

The procedure is basically the same for reupholstering any piece of stuffed furniture with conventional construction, such as the easy chair shown at top right. For a first project, however, it is best to avoid elaborate pieces in favor of one with simple lines. The work proceeds logically in sequence from seat to arms to inside back to outside back (Figure C).

Stripping the Seat Bottom
To begin stripping down a stuffed chair for reupholstering, turn the chair upside down on a pair of padded sawhorses. (Alternatively, fashion a padded work space by covering a table with blankets.) Using a mallet and chisel (one set aside for this purpose) or, preferably, an upholsterer's tack-pulling tool, remove the tacks or staples that hold the cambric that covers the bottom (photograph 16). If the chair has a flounce, remove it. Discard the old tacks as you remove them; so many will be bent they are not worth salvaging.

Beneath the cambric you will find a covering of burlap and a layer of woven jute webbing. Remove the burlap; then put a pencil line on each side of each piece of webbing where it is tacked to a rail, as a later guide in positioning replacement webbing. Remove the webbing to expose the bottoms of the springs. Discard the old burlap and webbing. (You can use the old burlap as a pattern in cutting new if you find that easier than measuring.)

Through the rewarding craft of reupholstery, a worn-out armchair has been restored to usefulness, comfort, and beauty. Other than its frame and coil springs, the chair is new from the inside out—and at a fraction of the cost of replacing it.

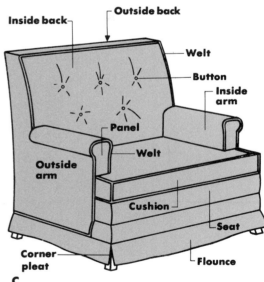

Figure C: These are the parts you are likely to encounter if you reupholster an easy chair of conventional coil-spring construction. In addition, the chair may have wings at the sides of the back. When you calculate your fabric needs, keep in mind that you need two of some pieces, such as the inside arm, the outside arm, and the panel. A chair like this requires about six yards of upholstery material.

16: To begin stripping an easy chair, turn it upside down on a padded sawhorse or table. Pry out the tacks holding the cambric cover, the flounce (skirt) if there is one, burlap, and the webbing under the springs. Discard tacks as you remove them.

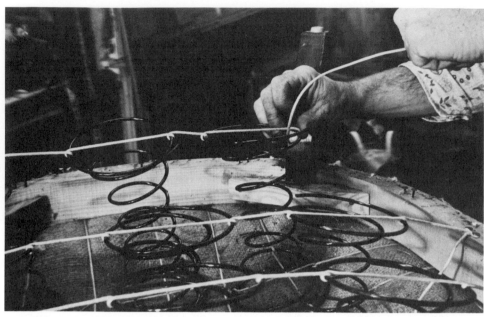

17: To repair a wobbly leg, it is best to pry it off, sand off the old glue, reglue the joint, and clamp until the glue is dry.

18: Working from side to side, loop the cord (anchored at one end as shown in Figure D) around both sides of each spring. Loop the free end of the cord around the second pair of tacks, but before you drive them all the way in, work the slack out of the cord by pressing on the springs as you pull on the cord.

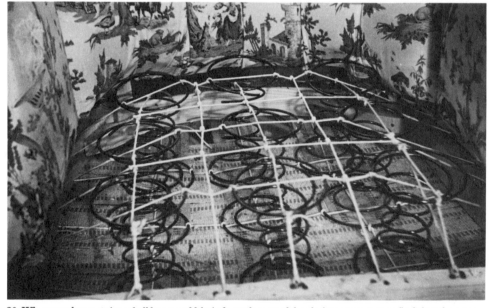

19: To complete the four-way tie of each spring, add front-to-back cords, but this time tie an overhand knot at each spring intersection, pulling the cord tight and straightening the spring before going on to the next knot.

20: When you have stripped all layers of fabric from the top of the chair seat, you may find that the tops of the springs also need retying. Follow the method used on the bottom of the springs, but use an overhand knot in both directions each time the cord crosses a spring. Add extra bridging rows between springs, knotting cords wherever they cross.

Repairing the Frame

Check the wooden frame for possible damage. If the legs are wobbly or the frame is split, those parts should be reglued. To firm an insecure leg, pry it off and scrape off the old glue. Sand the joining areas smooth. Apply white glue or furniture glue to the dowels, dowel holes, and adjacent areas. Reset the leg. Tap it in place with a hammer, and hold it with a clamp until the glue is dry (photograph 17). Small splits in the frame can also be glued and clamped. Larger splits need to be glued and pegged with a ¼-inch dowel. To do this, glue and clamp the split; then drill a ¼-inch hole diagonally through the split in the frame. Put glue in the hole, insert a dowel, and tap it into place with a hammer. A protruding end can be cut flush with the frame using a coping saw. White glue will dry in about six hours.

Tying the Spring Bottom

The next step is critical in building a comfortable foundation. Several springs may have broken loose from the jute cords that hold them in an equally spaced, upright position. If any of the cords are broken, it is possible that all are near the breaking point. All should be replaced. There are several ways to tie springs. I have found that a four-way tie, using jute spring twine, is a reliable method. First, cut the old cords loose, discard them, and remove the old tacks. Drive pairs of new 12-ounce tacks partway in, ½ inch apart, centered at the end of each row of springs on all four sides of the frame. Beginning at one side of the chair, at the center row of springs, loop the cord and pass the loop between the tacks. Flip the loop over so it runs outside the two tacks, as detailed in Figure D. Pull the cord tight and secure it by driving the tacks into the frame as far as they will go. Take the cord to the first spring in the row, and make a single turn around the near side and far side of the spring. In the same way, make single turns around the rest of the springs in turn until you reach the other side of the chair (photograph 18). Make the same flipped-over loop around a pair of tacks there. Before driving the tacks in, however, work slack out of the cord by pulling on it as you press down on the springs. If you loop the cord around the springs instead of tying it, you can adjust the springs to an upright position in a taut, straight line. Finally, secure the cord by hammering the tacks fully into place. Loop cords in the same way from side to side over the other rows of springs.

For the front-to-back rows of cord, a different system is used to tie the springs. The loop over a pair of tacks is the same. But instead of simply looping each spring wire as you come to it, make an overhand knot at each side of each spring, pulling the cord taut and putting the spring in an upright position before tightening each knot (photograph 19). At the end of the row of springs, repeat the loop around a pair of tacks and hammer them down.

Bottom Webbing

Using the pencil lines drawn on the frame earlier as guidelines, install a 3½-inch-wide length of jute webbing over the center row of springs, front to back. Allow an extra inch of webbing at the free end. Tack the free end of the webbing to the frame with a row of four tacks. Fold the 1-inch overlap back on itself, and tack it to the frame with four more tacks, staggering them so you do not hit the first tacks. Grip the webbing at the opposite side with a webbing stretcher. Push the stretcher down until the webbing is stretched as taut as possible. Tack it in place with four tacks. Cut off the webbing, again allowing a 1-inch overlap. Fold it back on itself and tack it again with four more tacks. Attach webbing across the other rows of springs, front to back, in the same way. Then attach the side-to-side bands, weaving them over and under the lengthwise bands. These bands should be tightly fitted together, side by side, with no space between them.

Stripping the Outside

Remove the old upholstery fabric from the outside back and sides, keeping as much of it intact as possible for use as a pattern in cutting the new cover. Carefully, remove the cotton padding and any horsehair stuffing. Save them for reuse. Pull out all tacks and staples from the frame. If the inside back has tufting buttons, their tie strings, tied to small cotton balls, will show at the back when the back fabric is removed. Cut the strings with a scissors and discard the cotton balls.

Retying the Top Springs

Remove the old burlap that covers the seat platform. That will expose the tops of the springs. Use a curved upholstery needle and nylon tufting twine to sew the bottom of each spring to the webbing in four places. Make a knot at each place to hold the springs securely. Since springs break loose at the top less often than at the bottom, the top ties may be in good condition. If the spring tops need retying, remove the old cords and tacks. Drive in pairs of tacks partway as you did on the bottom. Tie in new cords, but this time use overhand knots at each intersection with a spring, both lengthwise and crosswise. Then add pairs of tacks along the seat frame between the rows of springs for additional rows of bridge ties. With these, make overhand knots wherever one cord crosses another (photograph 20).

D

Figure D: To anchor the cord used for tying coil springs, first drive two 12-ounce tacks partway into the frame, ½ inch apart, at the end of a row of springs. Push a loop of jute cord between the tacks (left). Flip the loop over the tack heads (right), pull the cord tight, and finish driving in the tacks.

21: Cut a new oversized piece of burlap to cover the springs in the seat. Starting at the center of the front, tack opposite edges to the frame, working each time from the middle toward the corners and smoothing the burlap as you go.

22: Measure a length of fox edging to span the front of the seat. Tack it to the inside of the frame, not to the top edge, or sew it to the burlap with the curved upholstery needle. The edging holds seat stuffing in place and keeps the upholstery from wearing out because of rubbing against the frame.

23: Sew a 10-inch-wide strip of muslin to the burlap 5 inches back from the edge of the seat. Fold the muslin back and put several layers of cotton padding over the burlap between the fox edging and the front edge of the muslin.

24: Bring the loose end of muslin forward over the cotton padding. Pulling it tight, tack it to the front rail as shown and trim.

Upholstering the Seat

A cover is needed over the top of the springs to keep the stuffing from falling in or being torn. Measure the seat for new burlap or use the old piece as a pattern. The new piece should be 5 inches longer and wider than the old piece. Center the burlap over the springs. Tuck the overhanging edges through at the sides and back. A screwdriver makes a good pushing tool for this. Use three-ounce tacks to attach the burlap to the top of the seat frame (photograph 21). Work from opposite sides, beginning each time at the center and working to the outer corners. Make sure the burlap is pulled evenly from all sides. Make diagonal cuts as needed to fit around corners and curves. When the tacking is completed, trim off the excess burlap 1 inch outside the tacks. Fold this overlap back on itself and tack through it.

To protect the final covering from wear and to build up a front edge so the seat padding stays in place, a roll of fox edging (roll edging) is sewn or tacked across the seat between the front edge and the first row of springs (photograph 22). (Fox edging is a jute-covered roll of scrap paper; it can be bought by the foot.)

Next, a piece of muslin 10 inches deep and as wide as the seat is sewn to the burlap about 5 inches back from the front edge of the chair. Drape the muslin over the front edge and sew it with a curved needle and No. 252 jute or eight-ounce nylon tufting twine. Then fold back the muslin and lay several layers of cotton padding between the fox edging and the muslin seam (photograph 23). Do not tack the cotton padding down. Bring the unsewn end of the muslin forward over the cotton, pull it tight, and tack it to the front of the seat frame with three-ounce tacks. Trim off the excess muslin (photograph 24).

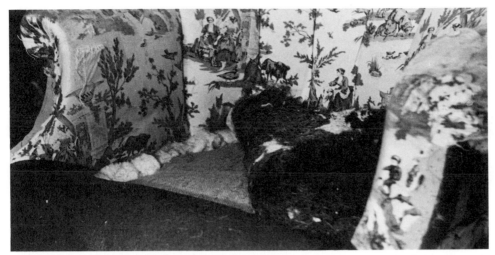

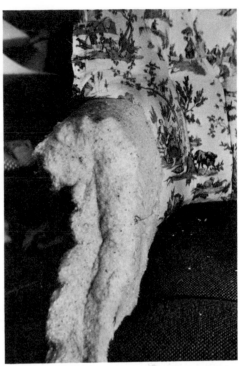

25: If you have salvaged, washed, and fluffed used horsehair, place it on the seat of the chair and cover it with a layer or two of cotton padding. If the seat seems too convex, put extra puffs of padding around the sides to build up the horsehair. If you do not have horsehair, use one or two layers of cotton padding.

27: Place cotton padding over the front panel of the stripped arm of the chair. Then lay a second piece that extends from just under the outside roll of the arm, across the top, and down the inside to a point where the arm meets the seat.

26: Lay the final covering on the seat and tack its front edge under the front of the frame. Push the side edges through between the arm and the seat, as you did with the burlap, and then tack them to the inside of the frame.

If you have horsehair available that you have salvaged, place a layer of it over the entire seat (photograph 25). Cover it with a layer or two of cotton padding. If you do not have horsehair, use one or two layers of cotton. Either may be covered with muslin, or you can cover it directly with the new upholstery fabric. If you choose the latter, measure and cut the fabric and attach it in the same way as you did the burlap (photograph 26). If the chair is not to be finished with a flounce at the bottom, take special care when you cut and tack the fabric around the legs. All tacks should be driven into the bottom edge of the frame.

Arms

Do each arm separately. Arm rests are usually subject to more wear than any other part of the chair, so it is usually necessary to replace matted arm padding with new padding (photograph 27). First remove the upholstery fabric covering the inside of the arm over the top to the outer side of the arm rest. Then remove the fabric from the front panel of the arm rest. If the fabric is too worn to serve as a pattern or comes off in small pieces, measure and cut patterns for these shapes. Then lay the new cotton padding in place.

Next, you need to cut the front panel of the arm. First pin a rectangular piece of muslin to the front of the arm. Outline its shape with colored chalk. Remove the pins and cut out the shape, following the chalk mark but allowing an extra 2 inches all around for error. Next, measure the piece that extends from the seat over the top of the arm by draping a piece of muslin up the inside arm, over the top, and down to a line just under the curve of the outside arm. Add a seam allowance of 2

28: Join the front panel of the arm to the inside arm piece with a length of welt (cord encased in a strip of upholstery fabric). Slip the joined pieces in place and tack them to the frame.

29: When the upholstery fabric has been fitted over the inside and the front of an arm, finish the front panel neatly on the outside with a cardboard tacking strip, pushed tight against the outer welt.

inches where this piece meets the front panel. Position the two muslin pieces on the arm again, and pin their edges together where they meet; then baste and machine or hand-sew them together. Turn the sleeve that results right side out and pull it over the arm, taking care not to dislodge the padding. Tack the muslin sleeve in place and trim off excess material.

Use the same procedure to fit and cut the upholstery material that goes over the muslin. But in this case, attach a length of welt (page 2657) to the front panel, machine-stitching it along the chalked line. Use sufficient welt to trim the front edge of the arm below the outside curve, but do not sew this part. Machine stitch the front panel and welt to the inside-arm fabric. Slip the assembled sleeve, right side out, over the arm and tack it in place (photograph 28). Upholster the other arm in the same manner. Attach cardboard tacking strips to the outside of both arms, flush against the welt, and trim off excess fabric (photograph 29).

Inside Back

Remove and discard any back buttons; because you clipped the cotton-anchored strings from the outside of the back earlier, they will pull off easily. Remove the old covering and use it as a pattern for cutting the new fabric. Examine the cotton padding. If there are worn spots, fill them with additional padding, but avoid making lumps that would be difficult to smooth out when the new fabric is attached. Fit the new fabric in place. A curved back is more difficult to fit than a straight back. (If necessary for a tight fit, you can cut 3-inch slits 3 inches apart along the bottom of the fabric, where it meets the seat.) Holding the fabric against the inside back, chalk a line at the bottom, following the curve of the seat.

Place the inside back fabric on a flat table. Cut off the material along the chalk line. Next, attach a pull strip of scrap material to the curved bottom that you can push through the opening between the inside of the back and the seat. This will result in a tight fitting, contoured covering for the inside back.

For the pull strip, you will need a 6-inch-deep strip of material, 8 inches wider than the inside-back fabric. Gather the pull-strip material to permit more freedom when you pull the fabric through; then machine sew the pull-strip to the fabric.

Drape the upholstery fabric over the inside back and push the pull strip through to the bottom using a screwdriver. Smooth the fabric to eliminate creases. Standing at the outside back of the chair, tack the upholstery fabric to the centers of both the top and bottom frames, using 6-ounce tacks. Check and smooth the fabric. Tack from the centers out to the edges. Check repeatedly as you continue to drive tacks.

Make slits in the inside-back fabric to fit it around the inside arms. Tuck these ends in place with a screwdriver.

The placement of buttons on the inside back is more functional than ornamental. Without them, the fabric and padding would lose their shape. The buttons take up any remaining slack in the fabric and hold it in place. Metal tufting buttons are sold in department stores. You can also have an upholsterer cover buttons in your own fabric; upholstery shops have special machines for this purpose.

Indicate a pattern for the button placement with pins. Thread a large straight needle with tufting twine or string. Attach the buttons with the strings protruding through the outside back. Tie these ends around wads of cotton (photograph 30). (Wads keep the knots from showing through the upholstery fabric.)

Tack welt along the top and sides of the inside fabric on the chair back as far down as the arms. Attach a cardboard tacking strip on the back, flush against the welt.

Outside Back and Front

Fit and tack burlap to the back from just inside the tacking strips to the bottom frame. Fit and tack cotton padding to the back. Cut the upholstery fabric and place it, reverse side up, draped over the top of the chair to the front. Tack the top of the fabric to the top rail of the chair (photograph 31). Attach a cardboard tacking strip across the same stretch of fabric, and tack a layer of cotton padding over the strip. Pull the reversed fabric over the back and tack it to the bottom edge of the bottom frame.

Upholster the sides the same way, following the sequence of burlap, cotton, blind tacking of fabric, cardboard tacking strip, cotton padding, and fabric. Using a curved upholstery needle, hand sew the outside arm fabric to the welting.

31: To cover the back, lay a measured piece of upholstery material, reverse side up, along the top of the chair, draped toward the front, and tack the edge in place. Tack a cardboard tacking strip over the tacks, and put cotton padding over the tacking strip; then fold the upholstery fabric back down over it.

30: Work out a pattern of tufting buttons for the inside back. Using needle and tufting twine, run stitches from the buttons through to the outside back, pulling each button sufficiently to create a tuft in front. Tie off each button thread around a wad of cotton to keep the knots from showing on the back. Trim excess string.

Turn the chair upside down and tack a piece of black cambric to the bottom. If a flounce is to be used to hide the legs, it should be lined with muslin. This will make the material easier to fit. With the chair in the upside-down position, stay-tack the skirt across the front. When held up against the leg, the skirt should expose ½ inch of the leg. Stay-tack the skirt along the other three sides and check each leg for clearance. Set the tacks in place. Attach the skirt with a tacking strip, using 12-ounce tacks.

Instead of a skirt, you may want to finish the bottom edge with gimp. Gimp is an ornamental trim tape available in a variety of colors and textures in department stores. It is used to cover fabric tacks around legs or exposed wooden areas. It can be attached with thin blue gimp tacks that are almost invisible, or with glue.

Re-covering a Seat Cushion
Cushions of old easy chairs are often stuffed with horsehair and many have coil springs. Do not attempt to restuff the cushion with horsehair or to retie the springs, since both of these operations require the use of a stuffing machine. Rather, make a new cushion starting with 4-inch-thick foam rubber. You can probably buy a foam cushion the right size and shape; if not, make a pattern by snugly fitting paper into the chair seat, matching the curves. Cut the pattern, and check its fit; then make a second pattern enlarged by ½-inch in both dimensions. By making it larger than the actual measurements, you allow for the proper compression when the foam is covered with fabric. Take your pattern to a foam-rubber supplier and have the foam cut there to insure that the sides will be vertical all around.

Adding a ¾-inch seam allowance, use the first pattern to cut out a fabric top and a bottom. Measure the perimeter of the sides of the cushion, and cut a strip that long and 4 inches wide, plus a ¾-inch allowance for each seam. Welting can be applied at the seams as they are stitched but it is not necessary. Stitch the top and bottom pieces to the side strip, leaving the top seam open at the back. Turn the cover right side out and stuff in the foam, smoothing the fabric as you go. Then hand stitch the top seam across the back. Professional upholsterers do not recommend the insertion of a zipper in an upholstered cushion.

For related entries, see "Antiquing Furniture," "Caning and Rushing," "Furniture Refinishing," "Gold Leafing," "Plastic Pipe Constructions," "Plywood and Foam Furnishings," "Rockers and Cradles," "Shaker Furniture," "Structural Furnishings," and "Tables and Benches."

VALENTINES
Messages of Love

Jill Barber has taught high-school art and has designed cards for UNICEF *and for Georg Jensen. Her "Season's Greetings" card for* UNICEF *was displayed as a poster in 6,000 store windows and was sold in Europe. Jill is also a sculptor; she studied in Lucca, Italy, and returns to Italy each summer to work and to buy marble. An exhibit of her sculpture was shown at Art Circle 74 in New York.*

One of the sweetest expressions of loving sentiment is the centuries-old custom of sending valentines on February 14. The custom becomes even more meaningful if your valentine is hand crafted, as are those described on pages 2672 through 2675. (All valentines were homemade until late in the eighteenth century, when the first commercial cards were printed in Germany and exported to England.)

The valentine holiday apparently stems from an ancient Roman ritual, the feast of Lupercalia, a festival that celebrated spring. The festival took place on February 15 because it was believed that birds mated at that time. In a lottery, each man drew the name of a woman who would be his partner during the festivities.

Patron Saint of Lovers

When the pagan festival was adopted by the Christians, it was renamed in honor of Valentinus, a priest who was beheaded on February 14 in the year 270 A. D. As St. Valentine, he is known as the patron saint of lovers due more to the date of his beheading than to a lifetime devoted to converting Romans to Christianity.

But the custom of drawing a valentine by lot continued into the eighteenth century. In England, Scotland, Italy, and the United States, the word valentine came to mean sweetheart. Robert Herrick, an English poet of the fifteenth century, wrote a poem, *To His Valentine, on St. Valentine's Day*. The practice of sending written valentines probably began in England, for in the English lottery, each man was supposed to send a note to his chosen one to tell her of his good fortune in having her name; then he would court her for a year. (Samuel Pepys' diary entry for February 14, 1661, tells of a note written to his wife by the man who had drawn her name—the lottery in England included the names of married people.)

Valentine customs remained the same through the middle of the eighteenth century, but the nature of the cards underwent some changes. The first homemade valentines consisted of verses and designs worked on printed and embossed writing paper. Those who could not compose their own verses could buy little books called valentine writers. These contained every type of verse from sentimental to comic to lewd. Such books appeared in America as early as 1723.

Commercial Valentines

Commercial valentines were first published in the United States around 1834 by Elton and Company, New York. In England about this time, commercial Victorian valentines were being introduced. They had a lace border with embossed edges and a hand-colored or lithographed picture in the center. The comic valentines of the period were rude and vulgar. These were often sent anonymously. Movable valentines—cards with tabs that could move a tongue, arm, or leg—became popular, although such cards were invented in Germany a century earlier.

Collectors consider the 1840s to be the golden age of the valentine. The quality of the lace paper, the embossed edges, and the colored designs used then have never been surpassed. The two people whose names are associated with these beautiful valentines are Jonathan King of London and Esther Howland of Worcester, Massachusetts. One of Esther Howland's innovations was to use colored paper behind the lace and embossed paper so the designs would be more prominent. The idea of making lace paper is credited to an Englishman by the name of Joseph Addenbrooke. Before 1840, paper to be embossed was laid on a die and hammered. Addenbrooke had the idea of filing off the raised part of the paper, thus creating a lacy effect.

By the late 1850s the elements of Victorian valentines—the lace paper, embossed paper, and colored cutouts—were being manufactured in Germany and left unassembled; anyone could order the parts and put them together himself.

The heart-shaped valentine, opposite, was created by Geno Sarturi of New York, from antique lace paper and colored cutouts. Surrounding it are antique valentines from Mr. Sarturi's collection. These are also pictured on pages 2668 through 2671.

This three-dimensional valentine was made in Germany in the 1890s. The card folds flat, but when opened it consists of four layers: the fence and flowers, the wheels of the carriage, the carriage, and the background. Mechanically easy to open, the card is perfectly balanced.

Antique Valentines
The antique valentines on these pages are from the collection of Geno Sarturi, owner of Brandon Memorabilia, a shop in New York. The shop sells antique greeting cards and posters, as well as materials for making valentines.

The Clerk.

You thump the typewriter passably well,
But what a pity you cannot spell,
You try to keep books, but sure as fate,
You cannot get your balance straight.
You're a good penman, you're apt to think,
But your paper and hands are stained with ink.
You cannot correctly transcribe a letter
Go get a job that suits you better

DON'T

TRY TO BE A MASHER, AND
STAND ON STREET CORNERS
TO OGLE GIRLS.
BE A MAN.

THE GRAFTER

Mr. All around Grafter, you're stuck on yourself,
For greed or for gold or for money or pelf,
You smile with that awful cigar in your face,
But the smile is a fake. You're a living disgrace.

LOST
CONSCIENCE
RETURN TO

Funny, satirical, and sometimes downright rude valentines have been popular for years. These three cards are American comic valentines of the 1890s that were reprinted in the 1920s. The center card, signed H, is the work of a man named Heller, famous for his comic valentines.

This Italian valentine postcard is a black-and-white photograph tinted with watercolors. The postcard is from the mid-1920s; its message says, "I sigh for you."

This coy little girl with a message for her sweetheart is an American mechanical valentine of the 1920s. A tab in the back of the card moves the girl's tongue, eyes, and ear. Mechanical cards were invented in eighteenth-century Germany.

The lace valentine (right) is an example of a card assembled in the United States from imported materials. The colored cutouts came from Germany, the lace paper from England. The card was assembled in the 1890s, and has a deeply scalloped border like valentines of this period.

Sweet hope doth fill
my breast to-day;
My love will grant
my wish I pray.

I wish my pen...
Had eloquence to tell
How much I love thee.
For I love thee well.

This silk-fringed valentine was made in the United States around 1880 with designs that were printed in Germany. The card has four different designs, two on the front and two on the back, all consisting of cupids with flowers. The silk fringe is caught between the two layers of paper. The card folds in the center and has silk tassels on either end.

This art-nouveau card was hand-painted in the United States. Although not dated, the card is assigned to the period between 1890 and 1910, when art-nouveau designs flourished. The card has a slightly three-dimensional effect created by the folded edges of the first flower border that surrounds the girl's picture.

This German postcard combines many popular valentine motifs: hearts, flowers, birds, and a cupid with a quiver full of arrows. The postcard was made around the turn of the century, definitely before 1907 because the back of the card is not divided into spaces for address and message, a custom started in 1907.

This lace valentine of the 1890s was assembled in the United States from cutouts from Germany and lace paper from England. The border creates a cameo effect.

A

Figure A: Trace this heart twice to make the two hearts that decorate the front of the five-language greeting card.

Paper Cutting and Folding
Name your heart

One way to express your love is to put your name and your loved one's name on two hearts. On the card shown below, the hearts are on a background of the word love, typed in five different languages. To make the card, you will need: a piece of red paper 6 by 8½ inches; a scrap of white paper at least 2 by 4 inches for silhouetting the hearts; rubber cement; and a transfer alphabet (available at an art supply store). To type the background words, you will need a typewriter.

Fold the red paper in half to make a 6-by-4¼-inch rectangle. From the extra piece of white paper, cut out two hearts, following Figure A. Move the two hearts around on the red paper until you are pleased with the placement. Using rubber cement only on the back of the hearts, glue them in place. Use only a little rubber cement because you will peel off the hearts after you type the background.

Place the unfolded card in the typewriter, but type across the front of the card only, starting at the fold mark. The word love is typed in English, French, Italian, Dutch, and German. The card reads *love, amour, amor, liefde, liebe*.

1: The background for the five-language card is made by typing across the card, over the hearts, glued on temporarily. When you peel off the hearts, the area beneath will be blank, ready to receive names.

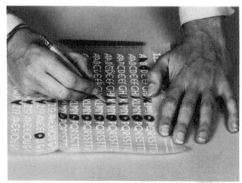

2: To use transfer type, place a letter where you want it to appear, and burnish the paper with a pencil or other blunt tool.

3: When you peel off the waxed paper or acetate with the letters on it, the letter you have rubbed will remain in place on the card.

A simply designed card has an international flavor because it says "love" in five languages: English, French, Italian, Dutch, and German. The names were added with transfer type.

Each word is typed repeatedly across one line. Type across the white hearts; the area beneath remains blank. When you have finished typing, peel off the white hearts (photograph 1). Rub a clean finger over the blank hearts to pick up any rubber cement remaining on the red paper. Using the transfer alphabet, put the names inside the hearts. Place one letter at a time in the appropriate place and rub the back of the letter firmly with a soft pencil or a letter opener (photograph 2). Then peel off the waxed paper or acetate and the letter will be transferred onto the card (photograph 3). When the names are on the hearts, you may want to add an ampersand between them. Write your message of love on the inside.

Paper Cutting and Folding
King and queen of hearts

You can let the king and queen of hearts from an old deck of playing cards represent you and your loved one, as shown on the valentine below. To make this card you will need: a piece of red paper 10 by 12 inches; a sheet of the special white paper used for correcting typewriter errors; pencil; ruler; masking tape; a felt-tipped marker; white glue; and cards picturing the king and queen of hearts.

Making the Design
To make the card, rule off the design area, a 6-by-4-inch rectangle, on the unfolded red paper. Tape a sheet of white correction paper over the design area, using masking tape kept outside of this area. Insert this sandwich into the typewriter, and type periods across the top row, with a space between each period. For the next row, start with a space, then a period, so the periods in this row will not be directly below the ones in the row above. Alternate rows down the front of the card.

Remove the card from the typewriter and take the white correction paper off the card (photograph 4). Shake the card to remove any loose powder left by the correction paper. Trim the card to a 6-by-8-inch rectangle; then fold to get a 6-by-4-inch card with the white dots on the front. Center the two playing cards on the front of the card, and trace around them with the felt-tipped marker. Cut out the king and queen motifs from the cards, and glue each in the center of a traced rectangle. Write a message to your king or queen on the inside of the card.

4: To make the background for the king-and-queen card, use white correction paper to type periods across the front of the card; then peel off the correction paper and trim the card to size.

With a pair of playing cards, you can proclaim yourselves the king and queen of hearts for Valentine's Day.

Lovebirds in a tree

With a heart emblazoned on each breast, two lovebirds in a tree are depicted on the card shown at lower left. To make the card, you will need: a 6¼-by-9-inch piece of green paper; a 3½-by-5-inch piece of black paper; small pieces of dark green, white, and red paper; and white glue. You will also need a paper punch to make the green dots that represent leaves on the tree.

B
Figure B: Trace the tree and the lovebirds for the green-background greeting card.

The Design
To make the card, fold the green paper in half to make a 6¼-by-4½-inch rectangle. Trace the tree in Figure B, cut it out of black paper, and glue it to the center of the front of the card. Trace the birds in Figure B and cut them out of white paper. Using the hole puncher, cut 40 to 50 dots out of dark-green paper. Glue the dots to the front of the card, clustering them around the branches of the tree. Then glue the lovebirds in place so they appear to be perched on branches. Cut out a tiny red heart for each bird and glue it in place. Then write your message on the inside of the card.

Valentine gift box

One special way to give a gift on Valentine's Day is to use a gift box that is a gift in itself. The one shown opposite consists of a clear plastic cube, available at variety stores and camera shops, with a decorated paper lining folded and placed inside. If you like, cut out one of the hearts on the cube lining and place a photograph of yourself behind the opening. The cube can be the box in which you place a gift for your special valentine.

To make a pattern for the paper cube, measure the inside dimensions of one side of the plastic cube. The cube pictured has sides 3 15/16 inches square. On pattern paper, draw six squares of this size, placing four in a vertical row and one on either side of the second square, as shown in Figure C. Cut out this cross shape and use it as a pattern to cut the same shape out of colored construction paper.

To decorate the colored paper, use circles and hearts cut out of colored paper and designs drawn with felt-tipped markers. When you draw straight lines with the marker, use a ruler, but put several pennies under the ruler to raise it so the marker ink won't flow onto the edge. Your design can continue from one side to another (photograph 5), or you can make different designs for each square. To assemble the paper cube, fold the cross-shaped paper on the fold lines. Then unfold, turn the paper over, and reinforce these five fold lines by putting masking tape on the reverse side. Put the folded paper cube into the plastic cube by inserting the short side first (photograph 6). The long side should be on top so you can open the paper cube. Slide the plastic top piece into place.

For related projects, see "Greeting Cards."

Two lovebirds sitting high in a tree make an attractive valentine motif. All the parts of this card are cut from colored paper and glued to a green background.

Hearts, disks, and bold stripes decorate this gift box. The decorated paper cube fits inside a clear plastic photograph cube.

5: The design on the cross-shaped colored paper can continue from one square to another. When folded, the design will turn a corner in the cube.

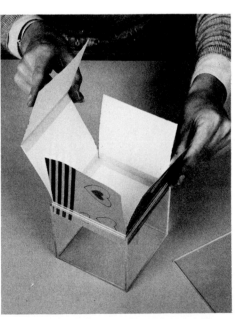

6: To assemble, fold the decorated paper so the short end forms an open cube as shown and insert this into the cube. Slide on the plastic top.

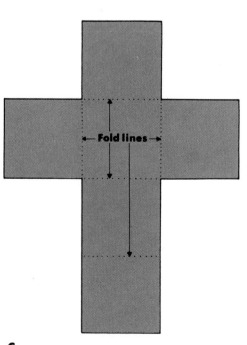

Fold lines

C
Figure C: To make a pattern for a paper cube, draw six squares as shown. Make each square the size of an inside wall of the plastic cube.

VEGETABLE DYES
Colors From Nature

Whether you are a knitter, a knotter, a weaver, a sewing enthusiast, or simply a lover of color, the ancient art of extracting dyes from plants can add a new dimension of craftsmanship to the things you make. Color has long been an essential aspect of fiber works; the use of natural dyestuffs dates back at least 50 centuries and is perhaps much older. But the accidental discovery in 1856 of a synthetic dye (in—of all things—coal tar) signaled the beginning of the end for the traditional dyer's craft. By the close of World War I, dyes of all colors had been synthesized, and only among craftsmen in remote areas did the ancient ways persist. The transition was swift and nearly total because the new dyes were predictable, convenient, and generally less costly, at least at the industrial level. If there was, as many dyers insist, a subtlety of color that only plants can give, its absence went unnoticed amid the zeal for progress.

Modern-Day Revival
Today, however, many craftsmen are returning to natural dyes, extracting color from plants over a kitchen range or an open fire. Some enjoy the ritual for the nostalgic visions it evokes; others simply prefer the colors. Nearly all agree that the home-brew experience is a delightful adventure, marked by constant surprises.

In fact, the renewed enthusiasm for natural dyes—despite their requiring a process that is sometimes laborious and always time-consuming—has sprung from the very cause of their demise a century ago; the difficulty of standardizing the result. Plant materials tend to yield offbeat, one-of-a-kind hues. No two dye batches ever come out exactly alike because there are so many variables involved—the time of year when the dyestuffs were harvested, their relative freshness and purity, the soil they grew in, the proportions of the recipes, the temperature and duration of steeping, and so on.

Sources of Plant Dyes
An added incentive for the home dyer is the wide availability of natural dyestuffs. No matter where you live, you probably have a cornucopia of raw materials nearby. Tomato vines, onion skins, marigolds, coffee beans, goldenrod, sunflowers, tea leaves, plantain, and scores of less well-known but equally abundant plant materials can be used for dyeing. In fact, there are very few plants that will not produce a dye. Anyone can develop a personal repertoire of colors; a chart of 85 dyestuffs and the colors they produce starts on page 2682. Note that a flower, leaf, root, or other plant part will not necessarily yield the expected color. Roses of all colors produce dyes in the tan-green-black range; silver-gray sagebrush gives browns, yellows, and greens; and from dull green tomato vines come red-browns and tans. But marigolds do indeed make gold dye.

Materials and Equipment
Once you learn the techniques of using natural dyes, you can use them to color raw fibers, yarn, cloth, finished fabric objects, macramé, crochet work, tie-dyed fabric, even leather, wood, and less likely substances. (Most natural dyes give their best color to wool.) The equipment you will need is simple and not expensive—a large enameled or stainless steel pot, a plastic bucket and measuring spoon, and a glass or wooden stirrer. Little space is needed. You can work with an outdoor fire, or a range in a well-ventilated kitchen. The amount of material you can dye at one time is limited only by the size of your pot and the quantity of dyestuffs you gather. However, most dyers find it convenient to limit their batches to one pound of fiber goods.

Nature's colors are yours for the gathering when you dye fleece, yarn, or fabric with plants that grow near you. Garden marigolds yielded the dye (in left-hand container) for the gold wool yarn that spills into the foreground. The other container holds logwood dye. Pokeweed yielded the brown skeins behind it—indigo, the blue. Beneath the bench are fabrics woven of fibers colored with natural dyes.

Alice Schlein has long been interested in textiles. "It's a family tradition," she says. Self-taught on the loom, she is a weaving instructor at the Museum School of Art in Greenville County, South Carolina, and a graduate of Douglass College. Among her special interests are wall hangings and hand-woven clothing.

Paint and Color
Making dyes colorfast

As anyone who has spilled red wine or blueberry sauce on a tablecloth knows, some natural substances yield permanent color all too readily. But most natural dyestuffs produce variable degrees of colorfastness. For this reason, dyers commonly add a step, and sometimes two, to the dyeing process to ensure color permanence. This consists of simmering the fibers or fabric to be dyed in a solution that causes a chemical bond to occur between dye and fiber. The solution is called a mordant, from an old word meaning to bite; the mordant was thought to bite into the structure of the fiber. Mordants have many forms: certain mosses, vinegar, ammonia, tannin, and other natural substances have long been used, but the most common mordants now used with natural dyes are alum, cream of tartar, and certain salts of chrome, copper, iron, and tin.

In addition to making dyes colorfast, the mordanting process often alters the colors that come from the dyestuff and the texture of the fiber itself. This can work for or against the dyer. Mordants are not interchangeable; with any one dyestuff each mordant produces a different result. For example, dahlia flowers used with a chrome mordant give an orange color, but with alum a light-yellow color. The color chart opposite shows approximately the results obtained from a few common dyestuffs combined with various mordants; the effect various mordants have on fibers is described below and opposite.

The mordant recommended for *all* the dye projects that follow is alum. I use alum most often because it is among the least hazardous and the easiest to use. As stressed on the following page, many other common mordants are very poisonous and must be used with extreme caution. But when you work with any chemical, and even with vegetable dyestuffs, exercise care. Fumes may be caustic; so do both mordanting and dyeing in a well-ventilated area—preferably outdoors. Always wear rubber gloves and an apron. When you prepare a solution, always add the chemicals to the water, not vice versa. And store all chemicals and solutions safely out of the reach of children.

With alum, it is usual to apply the mordant in a preliminary bath, then to dye the mordanted yarn in a second bath. This is not an absolute rule but it is a good one to follow at first. The mordant sometimes can be put in the dyebath when you are certain no adverse reaction will result. But when in doubt, mordant first; then dye in a separate bath. An additional mordant bath, after dyeing, is sometimes used to brighten or modify the color obtained.

About the Mordants

Alum (potassium aluminum sulfate) is a very good mordant to use in home dyeing because it is harmless except when ingested in large quantities. It comes in colorless or white crystals or powder. Three to four ounces are used for each pound of wool. Alum works best as a premordant and is good for all fibers. Its effect on color is generally slight. Because too much alum tends to make yarns sticky, it is often used with cream of tartar to maintain the softness of fibers.

Iron (ferrous sulfate), also called copperas or green vitriol, is another nontoxic mordant; it comes in pale-green crystals or powder. Recipes vary in calling for one-half to two ounces per pound of wool. The iron mordant bath is generally combined with the dye bath. Iron is not recommended for silk or coarse linen, as it darkens colors and adds a blue-purple-black hue. Too much iron streaks and injures fibers, producing a bronze color in black dye. A dyebath in an iron pot can be used in place of this chemical. Iron used with ammonia produces a greenish blue. These mordanted fibers must be thoroughly rinsed after use.

Tannin (tannic acid) occurs naturally in many dyestuffs, such as tea, oxgalls, and nutgalls, and, when it is present, it often obviates the need for any additional mordant. It is nontoxic and can be purchased as a light-brown powder. When tannin is used in chemical form, one or two ounces are mixed per pound of wool. It is generally used as a premordant or in the dyebath. Because tannin is light sensitive, fibers mordanted in it tend to darken with age; store tannin in a light-tight container.

Hazardous Mordants

The mordants that are hazardous and should be used only by experienced dyers include: chrome (potassium dichromate), a corrosive poison and a caustic skin irritant with highly toxic fumes; copper (cupric sulfate), also known as blue vitriol, very toxic in all forms; and tin (stannous chloride), very toxic with fumes that may irritate eyes and sinuses.

Additional Chemical Uses

Other chemicals used in vegetable dyeing include white vinegar, cream of tartar, baking soda, and ammonia. White vinegar is nontoxic and can be purchased at a grocery store. When added to a violet or purple dye, it turns the color red. Cream of tartar is nontoxic and can be purchased at a grocery store or, in larger quantities, from a chemical supplier. It is used to maintain the softness of fibers when an alum or tin mordant is used. Keep the lid tightly closed. A by-product of wine making, it is a whitish or reddish crystalline powder, depending on what kind of grapes it was made from. Baking soda is a nontoxic grocery or drugstore item. Added to violet or purple dyes, it produces a blue color. Ammonia is the familiar, but toxic, grocery or hardware store item. Only the clear, nonsudsy, nondetergent ammonia is used. It brings out the color of grasses and lichens, and sharpens yellows and greens.

Containers and utensils

Certain metals, including iron, tin, aluminum, and copper, will react chemically with many dyes and mordants. Hence the metals sometimes affect the color obtained. So unless a special effect is sought, use only tools and utensils made of chemically neutral materials. These include stainless steel, enamel, glass, ceramics, wood, and most plastics. Naturally, wood and plastic containers are not used near a heat source.

How Mordants Contribute to Dye Colors

As the chart below illustrates, each mordant has a distinct and generally predictable effect on dye colors. The colors shown are those that commonly result when one of the seven dyestuffs—selected at random—is used in combination with one of three mordants. (Blank spaces represent combinations that are unlikely or undesirable.) Some of the mordants are hazardous; for more information about them, see Hazardous Mordants, above.

DYESTUFFS		MORDANT		
Common Name	Latin Name	Alum	Iron	Tannin
Cockleburs	Xanthium (various)			
Goldenrod	Solidago (various)			
Logwood	Haematoxylon campechianum			
Safflower	Carthamus tinctorius			
Sassafras	Sassafras (various)			
Sedge	Carex (various)			
Sunflower	Helianthus (various)			

Mordanting Wool Yarn with Alum

It is hard to duplicate a color exactly, so you should mordant and dye all the wool yarn you will need for any one project at one time. To mordant one pound of yarn, you will need: small packages of alum and cream of tartar; water (preferably soft); a 5-gallon enameled or stainless steel cooking pot; scale and measuring spoon; a glass or wooden rod for stirring; a kitchen range, or fuel for an outdoor fire; and a plastic tub or bucket for rinsing.

Begin by skeining the yarn into a loose coil, about a foot in diameter. You can do this by winding it around your right hand and elbow. I use a collapsible reel, called a swift, available from weaving supply companies. To skein yarn on a swift, tie one end to any X-intersection on the reel (photograph 1), and rotate the device to wind the wool (photograph 2). When the skein is completed (limit the size to about four ounces for easy handling), tie the beginning and end strands together, and then loosely tie the skein in three or four places with 4-inch lengths of cotton string, securely knotted (photograph 3). Loosen the pin on the swift's handle, and the reel will contract, freeing the skein.

Preparing the Yarn

Wash the skeins of yarn in cold water and detergent; then thoroughly rinse them. I recommend soft water for all vegetable dyeing processes (minerals in hard water often darken colors). Rainwater is best, or you can use a commercial water softener in tap water as necessary.

To prepare the mordant bath, weigh out four ounces of alum for coarse yarns or three ounces for more delicate fibers, and one ounce of cream of tartar. I use a postal scale for this (photograph 4)—the quantities need to be fairly accurate. Alternatively, two level tablespoonfuls, loosely packed, are about one ounce of granular alum or cream of tartar. Dissolve the alum and the cream of tartar in a quart of cold water. Nearly fill a 5-gallon enameled container with cold water. Add the dissolved chemicals and stir well.

1: For skeining yarn, a special collapsible reel—appropriately named a swift—is a great help. The reel is made of wooden bars, which form a series of crosses. To skein yarn, first tie the end of the yarn to one of the crosses.

2: Hold the yarn in your right hand, and rotate the swift with your left hand, like a ferris wheel on its axis. The yarn will form a coil in the central channel. Guide it and loosen snarls with your left hand as necessary.

3: When you have coiled about four ounces of wool, tie both ends of the strand together, and encircle the skein in three or four places with loose loops securely knotted. To remove the skein, collapse the swift by loosening the pin on the handle.

Set the pot over heat and add the wet yarn. Raise the temperature of the mordant bath gradually to the simmering point, stirring the yarn from time to time (photograph 5). The proper steeping temperature, about 190 degrees Fahrenheit, will be reached when tiny bubbles start to appear on top of the liquid. Maintain this temperature for one hour by adjusting the heat. Never let the water boil. For tips on controlling outdoor fires, see below.

As the heated liquid evaporates, add more hot water as needed to maintain the level and temperature of the mordant bath. When the hour is nearly up, let the fire die down. When you can safely handle the pot with potholders, set it aside. Allow the bath to cool by itself. (Never change the temperature of wool suddenly.) When the bath is cool enough to be comfortable for a gloved hand—this usually takes about half an hour—remove the yarn from the mordant and gently squeeze out excess liquid (photograph 6).

The yarn is now ready to be dyed. You can begin immediately, or wrap the damp yarn loosely in a bath towel, store it in a cool place, and dye it the next day.

Outdoor fires

An outdoor dye or mordant bath over an open fire requires constant attention. You must add dry logs to the fire at just the right moment so the temperature does not fluctuate greatly. Add wood at the first sign of a weakening blaze; it will take time for the new wood to release its heat. It takes about a dozen fireplace logs to fuel the fire for an hour.

A simple and practical arrangement for simmering is to set the pot on a large grill supported by piles of loose bricks (stacked four or five high as shown in photograph 5). Put extra bricks on top of the grill to hold it securely. Center the fire under the grill; if it gets too hot, move the pot to one side away from the greatest heat. Construct your fireplace in an open area, downwind from the house and a safe distance away.

If you use a kitchen range for dyeing, remember that dyeing and mordanting fumes might be caustic; good ventilation is an essential precaution.

4: To prepare the mordant bath, measure the proper quantities of chemicals on a small postal scale, using a plastic or stainless steel spoon. Cover the scale with waxed paper to prevent contamination.

5: Immerse the wet yarn in the mordant bath, and bring the bath to the simmering point. Stir from time to time, so the mordant will penetrate the yarn fibers evenly. Use a wooden or glass stirring rod and a gentle, back-and-forth motion.

6: When the mordant bath has cooled sufficiently to be comfortable, put on rubber gloves and remove the yarn, squeezing out excess liquid. But do not wring the skein too hard, because this might damage the fibers.

85 NATURAL DYESTUFFS

Common name	Scientific name	Color	Mordant	Fibers	Permanence	Part or form	Best time	Condition
Acorns	Quercus (various)	Tan	Alum	Wool, silk	Excellent	Whole nut	Autumn	Fresh or dry
Alkanet	Alkanna tinctoria	Blue-gray	None	Wool	Good	Roots	(Purchase)	Dry
Annatto	Bixa orellana	Orange	Alum	Wool, silk	Fair	Seeds	(Purchase)	Dry
Apple, crab	Malus (various)	Pink	Alum	Wool	Fair-poor	Fruit	When mature	Fresh
Barberry	Berberis (various)	Tan	Alum	All	Excellent	All but roots	When mature	Fresh or dry
		Gray-black	Iron	Jute	Excellent			
Beet	Beta (various)	Tan	Alum	Wool, silk	Good-fair	Roots	When mature	Fresh
Birch, yellow	Betula lutea	Yellow-tan	Alum	Wool	Good-fair	Leaves	Spring	Fresh or dry
Blackberries	Rubus (various)	Purple-brown	Alum	Wool, silk	Fair	Fruit	When ripe	Fresh or frozen
Bloodroot	Sanguinaria canadensis	Orange	None	Wool, silk	Good	Roots	Summer	Fresh or dry
Broom sedge	Andropogon virginicus	Yellow-green	Alum	Wool	Good	All but roots	Summer	Dry
		Gold	Alum + tannin	Cotton	Good			
Butterfly weed	Asclepias tuberosa	Yellow	Alum	All	Good	Blossoms	When mature	Fresh
Butternut	Juglans cinerea	Brown	Alum	Wool	Good	Hulls	When ripe	Fresh or dry
		Green-tan	Alum	Cotton	Fair			
Catechu	Acacia catechu	Rust	None	All	Excellent	Resin or heartwood	(Purchase)	Dry
		Brown	Alum	All	Excellent			
Chamomile	Anthemis tinctoria	Buff	Alum	Wool	Fair	Flowers	When mature	Dry
Charcoal		Gray	Iron	Cotton, linen	Good	Any form	Any time	Dry
Chrysanthemum	Chrysanthemum (various)	Yellow	Alum	Wool, silk	Good	Flowers	When mature	Fresh or dry
Clay	Terra cotta	Tan-red brown	Alum	Wool, cotton	Good	Potters' clay	(Purchase)	Wet or dry
Cochineal (insect)	Dactylopius coccus	Purple-red	Alum	All	Good	Powder	(Purchase)	Dry
Cockleburs	Xanthium (various)	Brass	Alum	Silk, cotton	Excellent	Burrs	Autumn	Fresh
		Dark green	Iron	Wool	Good			
Coffee	Coffea arabica	Tan	Alum	All	Good	Beans, grounds	(Purchase)	Dry
Coreopsis	Coreopsis (various)	Orange-red	Alum	Wool	Good	Flowers	When mature	Fresh
Cotton	Gossypium (various)	Yellow-tan	Alum	Wool	Good	Flowers	When mature	Dry
		Yellow-tan	Alum + tannin	Cotton	Good			
Crocus	Crocus vernus	Turquoise	Alum	Wool	Good	Purple flowers	Spring	Fresh
Cudbear	Rocella (various)	Red	Alum	All	Excellent	Powder	(Purchase)	Dry
Cudweed	Gnaphalium (various)	Yellow	Alum	Wool	Good	Whole plant	When mature	Fresh
		Green	Alum + iron	Wool	Good			
Daffodil	Narcissus pseudonarcissus	Yellow	Alum	Wool	Good	Flowers	When mature	Fresh
Dahlia	Dahlia (various)	Yellow	Alum	Wool, silk	Good	Flowers	When mature	Fresh or dry
Dandelion	Taraxacum officinale	Yellow	Alum	Wool, silk, cotton	Good	Flowers	When mature	Fresh
Day lily	Hemerocallis (various)	Yellow	Alum	Wool, silk	Good-fair	Flowers	When mature	Fresh
Dock (wild rhubarb)	Rumex (various)	Tan	Vinegar	Wool, cotton	Good	Roots	Late summer	Fresh
		Green-gold	Ammonia	Wool, cotton	Good			
Elderberries	Sambucus canadensis	Purple	Alum	Wool, silk	Good	Fruit	When ripe	Fresh or frozen
Foxglove	Digitalis purpurea	Chartreuse	Alum	Wool	Good	Flowers	When mature	Fresh
Fustic	Chlorophora tinctoria	Yellow	Alum	All but linen	Excellent	Bark	(Purchase)	Dry
Goldenrod	Solidago (various)	Gray-green	Iron	Cotton, linen	Good-fair	Flowers	When mature	Fresh
Grapes, wild or concord	Vitis (various)	Lavender	Alum	All	Fair	Fruit	When ripe	Fresh
Gumweed	Grindelia (various)	Gold	Alum + ammonia	Wool	Good	Flowers/pods	When mature	Fresh
		Olive green	Alum + iron	Wool	Good			
Hedge nettle	Stachys (various)	Chartreuse	Alum	Wool	Good	Whole plant	When mature	Fresh
Herb robert	Geranium robertianum	Brown	Alum	Wool	Good	Whole plant	When mature	Fresh
Hickory	Carya laciniosa	Tan	Alum	All	Good	Hulls	Early autumn	Fresh or dry
Indigo	Indigofera (various)	Blue	Alum	All but linen	Excellent	Powder	(Purchase)	Dry
Knotweed	Polygonum aviculare	Cream yellow	Alum	Wool	Good	Whole plant	When mature	Fresh
Lichen, oak	Parmelia perlata	Pink-magenta	None	Wool	Good	Whole lichen	Any time	Fresh or dry
Lichen, rock	Parmelia sulcata	Magenta	None	Wool	Fair	Whole lichen	Any time	Fresh or dry
Lily of the valley	Convallaria majalis	Yellow-green	Alum	Wool, silk	Good	Leaves	Summer	Fresh

Common name	Scientific name	Color	Mordant	Fibers	Permanence	Part or form	Best time	Condition
Logwood	Haematoxylon campechianum	Dark purple	Alum	All	Good	Heartwood	(Purchase)	Dry
		Gray-blue	Iron	Wool	Good			
Madder	Rubia tinctorum	Red	Alum	All	Excellent	Root, powder	(Purchase)	Dry
Mallow	Malvia (various)	Blue	Alum	Wool	Good	Flowers	When mature	Fresh
		Khaki green	Alum + iron	Wool	Good			
Maple, Norway	Acer platnoides	Rose-tan	Alum	Wool	Good-fair	Bark	Spring	Fresh or dry
		Gray-drab	Alum + tannin	Cotton	Good			
Marigold	Tagetes (various)	Yellow-gold	Alum	Wool, silk	Good	Flowers	When mature	Fresh or dry
Mayweed	Anthemis cotula	Deep gold	Alum	Wool	Good	Whole plant	When mature	Fresh
Meadow rue	Thalictrum polycarpum	Yellow	Alum	Wool	Good	Whole plant	When mature	Fresh
Mulberry	Morus (various)	Gray-lavender	Alum	Wool	Fair	Fruit	When ripe	Fresh
Mullein	Verbascum thapsus	Yellow	Alum	All	Excellent	Leaves/stems	Autumn	Fresh or dry
Onion, red or yellow	Allium (various)	Burnt orange	Alum	Wool, cotton	Fair	Skin	When mature	Dry
Oregon grape	Mahonia (various)	Buff-tan	Alum	Wool	Fair	Root	Autumn	Fresh
Osage orange	Maclura pomifera	Yellow-tan	Alum	Wool	Good	Heartwood	Any time	Fresh or dry
Owl's clover	Orthocarpus (various)	Lemon yellow	None	Wool	Good	Whole plant	When mature	Fresh
		Yellow-gray	Alum + iron	Cotton	Good			
		Brass-khaki	Alum + iron	Wool	Good			
Peach	Prunus persica	Yellow	Alum	Wool, silk	Good	Leaves	Autumn	Fresh
Pigweed	Amaranthus (various)	Moss green	Alum	Wool	Good	Whole plant	When mature	Fresh
		Forest green	Alum + iron	Wool	Good			
Plantain	Plantago lanceolata	Dull gold	Alum	Wool	Good	Whole plant	When mature	Fresh
Pokeweed	Phytolacca americana	Red	Alum	Wool, silk	Good	Berries	When ripe	Fresh or dry
		Pink	Alum	Cotton, linen	Good			
Privet	Ligustrum (various)	Tan	Alum	All	Good	Leaves/twigs	Summer	Fresh
		Dark green	Iron	Wool	Good			
Rabbit brush	Chrysothamnus (various)	Lemon yellow	Alum	Wool	Good	Flower heads	When mature	Fresh or dry
Ragwort	Senecio jacobaea	Bright yellow	Alum	Wool	Good	Flower heads	When mature	Fresh
Rose	Rosa floribunda	Tan	Alum	All	Good	Leaves	Summer	Fresh
		Green-black	Iron	Wool, cotton	Good			
Rose	Rosa multiflora	Tan	Alum	Plant fibers	Excellent	Leaves	Summer	Fresh
		Black-gray	Iron		Good			
Safflower	Carthamus tinctorius	Yellow-tan	Alum	Wool, silk	Good	Powder	(Purchase)	Dry
		Brass	Iron	Wool	Good			
Sagebrush	Artemisia tridentata	Bright yellow	Alum	Fleece	Good	All but roots	When mature	Fresh
		Yellow	None	Raffia, reed	Good			
		Sage green	Alum + iron	Wool	Good			
		Brown	Iron	Raffia	Good			
Sassafras	Sassafras (various)	Red-tan	Alum	Wool, silk	Good	Leaves, bark	Summer	Fresh or dry
		Black-gray	Iron	Plant fibers	Good			
Scarlet sage	Salvia splendens	Pink	Alum	Wool, silk	Good-fair	Flowers	When mature	Fresh
		Tan	Iron	Cotton, linen	Good			
Seaweed	Rhodymenia (various)	Tan	Alum	Wool, silk	Good	Whole plant	Any time	Fresh
		Yellow-green	Iron	Wool	Good			
Sedge	Carex (various)	Yellow-green	Alum	All	Excellent	Grass	Summer	Fresh or dry
Self-heal	Prunella vulgaris	Bright olive	Alum	Wool	Good	Flowers	When mature	Fresh
Staghorn moss	Lycopodium clavatum	Green-yellow	None	Silk, wool	Good	Whole plant	Any time	Fresh
Sunflower	Helianthus (various)	Yellow-tan	Alum	Wool	Good	Seeds	When mature	Dry
		Gray-blue	Iron	Wool, cotton	Good			
Tarweed	Madia (various)	Yellow	Alum	Cotton, jute	Good	Whole plant	When mature	Fresh
Tea, black	Camellia sinensis	Rose-tan	Alum	All	Good	Leaves	(Purchase)	Dry
Tobacco	Nicotiana (various)	Brown	Alum	All	Good	Leaves	Summer	Fresh or dry
Tomato	Lycopersicon (various)	Red-brown	None	Wool, silk	Good	Vines	Summer	Fresh
		Tan	Alum	Wool, silk	Good			
Turmeric	Curcuma longa	Yellow	Alum	All	Good-fair	Powder	(Purchase)	Dry
Walnut, black	Juglans nigra	Brown	Alum	All	Excellent	Hulls	Late summer	Fresh or dry
		Black-gray	Iron	All	Excellent			
Weld	Reseda luteola	Yellow	Alum	Silk, wool	Excellent	All but roots	Late summer	Fresh or dry
Wood sorrel	Oxalis (various)	Maize	Alum	Jute, cotton	Good	Flowers	When mature	Fresh
Yarrow	Achillea millefolium	Maize	Alum	Wool	Good	Blooms/leaves	Any time	Fresh
		Dark green	Alum + iron	Wool	Good			
Zinnia	Zinnia (various)	Yellow	Alum	Wool, silk	Good	Flowers	When mature	Fresh or dry

Paint and Color
Dyeing wool yarn

There are hundreds of widely available natural dyestuffs that you may want to try. The three I selected to introduce natural dyeing are marigolds, black-walnut hulls, and logwood. The result of my day's dyeing is shown in photograph 15 (page 2686). With these general instructions, you will be able to improvise similar recipes with other dyestuffs.

With some plant materials, such as the black-walnut hulls, mordanting in advance is not necessary. In such cases a natural mordant—usually tannin—is contained in the dyestuff, so mordanting takes place automatically. But unless you use a mordant-bearing dye plant (see table, pages 2682 and 2683), do not begin dyeing until you have produced a quantity of mordanted yarn (pages 2678 through 2681).

The recipes that follow are for dyeing one pound of wool yarn. You can dye other quantities by adjusting the proportions. Or you can use the same ingredients to dye like quantities of woven fabric, whether of wool or other fibers. The recipes will produce acceptable, if different, shades on other fibers. There is an exception. Marigold dye is not recommended for use on linen or cotton. In addition to the

Animal, vegetable, or mineral?

The terms vegetable and natural, when applied to dyes, are often used interchangeably, but natural dyes are not all plant derivatives. A few natural dyes come from the animal and mineral kingdoms. Cochineal, a red dye, is extracted from an insect (*Dactylopius coccus*) that lives on cactus plants in Latin America. It takes 70,000 of the tiny insects to make a pound of cochineal dye. Tyrian purple, the color worn by the nobility of ancient Greece and Rome, was extracted from shellfish of the eastern Mediterranean. So costly was the dyestuff that even if commoners had not been forbidden to wear it, few could have afforded it. A few mineral pigments, such as iron buff and terra-cotta, are extracted from the earth.

7: Harvest flowers like these marigolds, or berries of dye plants, in late summer or when they reach their peak of maturity. For best results, use them immediately. If you experiment with unfamiliar plants, wear gloves. Barks and leaves for dyeing are usually gathered in spring, roots in autumn, heartwood at any time.

materials used in mordanting, you will need: a noncorroding colander; a 5-gallon plastic tub or pail; and the dyestuffs.

Dyeing with Fresh Marigolds

Any of the common marigold varieties can be used to produce a yellow or gold dye for wool or silk. The variety you use will largely determine the shade achieved. Different marigold varieties—and even different yellow-bearing plants, such as chrysanthemums—may be mixed. For best dye results, harvest the flowers when they are in full bloom (photograph 7), and use them immediately. If this is inconvenient, you can dry them in the sun or in a warm oven and use them later. (If you use another dye plant, check the table on pages 2682 and 2683 to see if it must be used fresh.) To dye one pound of wool yarn, you will need three-quarters of a pound of marigold flowers. (This is an exception to the general rule that you use two to three parts of fresh dyestuff to one part of textile or fiber.)

Place the marigolds and four gallons of water in the dye pot (photograph 8), and simmer them for an hour at about 190 degrees Fahrenheit, stirring occasionally to make sure all the flowers are immersed. Faster but less effective is to boil the dyestuff for 15 minutes. Generally dyes can be extracted from fresh plant matter by either of these methods.

When the solution has cooled, strain out all vegetable material to prevent it from fouling the wool later. One way to do this is to pour the contents of the pot through a colander into a second container (photograph 9). Rinse the dye pot with clear water; then pour the dye solution back into the pot. Add cold water until the pot is three-quarters full. When the solution is cool, add the mordanted yarn (photograph 10). If the yarn has begun to dry, moisten it before you place it in the pot. Turn on the range or build up the open fire and gradually bring the dyebath to the simmering point. This should take about half-an-hour. Keep the pot simmering for about an hour more, or until the yarn is the desired color.

Remove the pot from the fire and let the dyebath cool until the temperature is comfortable for a gloved hand. You can hasten the cooling process by adding a little cool water every few minutes (photograph 11). When the bath is cool, remove the yarn from the pot (photograph 12). Rinse it in successive water baths until the water remains clear. Squeeze out the excess water but do not wring. Hang the dyed yarn in the shade to dry.

8: To make a dyebath, place the dyestuff in four gallons of water and simmer for one hour. Stir occasionally to ensure an even extraction of color, especially when you work with buoyant dyestuffs.

9: To separate the liquid dye from the vegetable residue, pour the contents of the dye pot through a colander or other strainer and into another container. You may need to strain the mixture twice.

10: Let the dye solution cool; then add as much cold water as is needed to restore the four-gallon level. Put the premoistened, mordanted yarn into the pot before you reheat the dye.

11: After simmering for an hour, remove the dyebath from the heat and let it cool. To hasten cooling, add a little cold water every few minutes, but do not let the bath cool abruptly.

12: With hands gloved, remove the dyed yarn as soon as the liquid is comfortably cool. Rinse it repeatedly until the rinse water remains clear. Squeeze out excess water, but do not wring.

Dyeing with Black-Walnut Hulls

Black-walnut hulls have long been used as a dyestuff. A sixteenth-century Venetian dyer's manual gives several recipes for using them, including one for darkening skin. The hulls produce a range of warm tones, from beige to dark brown. For a deep color, use fresh hulls gathered in late summer, when the green outer covering becomes spotted with brown. For tan and beige tones, use dried hulls, brownish black in color. In this form, hulls are often used as an over-dye to take the bright edge away from colors obtained from other plants—a process known as saddening.

When you use walnut hulls, mordanting is unnecessary unless used to alter the color. A natural mordant in the dyestuff provides sufficient colorfastness; in fact, the color tends to darken with age. This dye works well on wool, silk, mohair, raffia, and other fibers.

To prepare enough dye for one pound of wool yarn, soak two to three pounds of dried black-walnut hulls in one gallon of water for 24 hours; then cut them into small

Keeping records

Many vegetable-dye enthusiasts keep detailed records of their experiments. A dye notebook or index file is invaluable in recalling how a color was achieved. For such records, the categories on pages 2682 and 2683 provide a useful place to start. Include a sample of the dye plant (or a drawing or photograph of it). Tape or staple a sample of the dyed yarn to the page where it is described. If more than one mordant was used, or if the time in the dye pot was not the same for all the skeins, include and label a sample of each result. List the exact proportions of the ingredients used—the dyestuff, mordants, other chemicals, water, and yarn. Also record the time and temperature used to extract the dye solution as well as to dye the yarn. Record technical data as you work; they are easily forgotten. Don't be selective. In a notebook, failures are as noteworthy as successes. Other information to include is the date and place the dyestuff was gathered, and the date when it was used (if different). After some time, assess the dye's colorfastness.

13: If you are using a relatively large source of dye color, such as soaked walnut hulls, cut the material into small pieces about the size of a bottle cap. This will let more dye be drawn into the bath.

14: From time to time, lift the yarn out of the dyebath with a long wooden stick so you can examine the color achieved. Wet wool will look slightly darker than when it is dry.

15: Hang dyed wool to dry in a shady place. A stick suspended between two chair backs makes a convenient drying rack, as does a clothesline (page 2688).

pieces (photograph 13). Put the pieces and the soaking water in a 5-gallon enamel dye pot, adding enough water to fill the pot three-quarters of the way to the top. Simmer for an hour or longer. If the hulls seem ready to disintegrate and foul the wool, remove them with a noncorrosive spoon or tongs. This probably will not be necessary; usually it is preferable to leave them in the bath to produce more color.

Allow the dyebath to cool; then add enough cold water to replace what has been lost in evaporation. Moisten the wool and put it in the cool dyebath; then slowly heat to the simmering point again. Simmer for an additional hour or until the desired color intensity is reached. The wool will lighten slightly as it dries. If you are dyeing more than one skein of yarn, you can achieve gradations of color by removing the skeins at intervals from the pot. Use a noncorrosive implement to fish them out, and be careful not to burn yourself. Techniques of cooling, rinsing, and drying are the same as for marigold dyeing (pages 2684 and 2685).

Dyeing with Logwood

Chipped or pulverized heart of logwood, from a tree that grows in the West Indies and Central America, has been used as a dye at least since the sixteenth century. It can be purchased at little cost from dye-supply houses and laboratory suppliers (logwood is also used in the preparation of microscope slides).

The quantity of logwood chips or powder you use should equal one-quarter to one-third the weight of the wool you intend to dye. Logwood is exceptionally rich in dye (the general formula is one or two parts of other woody dyestuffs to each part of yarn). Soak the logwood in water overnight. Then boil it vigorously for an hour. Remove all traces of the dyestuff from the bath, straining it through a colander if necessary (photograph 9, page 2685). When the bath is cool, put in the moist, alum-mordanted yarn and additional water, if necessary, until the pot is three-quarters full. Slowly heat the bath to simmer. Check the color of the yarn frequently (photograph 14), lifting it from the bath with a wooden stick. Logwood dye acts quickly; 15 to 30 minutes of simmering usually produces a deep purple.

Cool, rinse, and dry the yarn (page 2685). A convenient drying arrangement for the day's work, a dowel suspended between two chairs, is shown in photograph 15. If you wish, save the logwood-dye in a sealed glass container for future use.

Post Mordanting and Over Dyeing

It occasionally happens that the color achieved by a single mordanting and dyeing sequence leaves something to be desired. If this happens, you can modify the results with a second mordant bath. Tin is commonly used as an after-mordant to brighten the color (it imparts a red-to-yellow hue). Similarly, you can use a second dyebath in beige or gray to darken a tone. Or a second color can be introduced to change the first color entirely, as when a blue yarn is bathed in yellow dye to produce a blue-green or green yarn.

No special cleanup procedures are necessary. When you finish working, scour the utensils with household cleansers and rinse them thoroughly. But do not use the dyeing utensils for food preparations, and make sure you have stored the mordants and dyes safely.

For related projects and crafts, see "Batik," "Color Psychology," "Leather Working," "Raffia and Straw," "Spinning," "Tie Dyeing," and "Weaving."

Wools dyed with logwood, marigold, cochineal, and madder were woven into this vest.

Bibliography

Ancient Dyes for Modern Weavers by Palmy Weigle, Watson-Guptill Publications.
Dye Plants and Dyeing: A Handbook, edited by Ethel Jane McD. Schetky and others, Brooklyn Botanic Garden.
The Dye-Pot by Mary Frances Davidson, published by the author.
Dyes from Plants by Seonaid Robertson, Van Nostrand Reinhold Company.
Natural Dyes and Home Dyeing by Rita J. Adrosko, Dover Publications, Inc.
Natural Dyes in the U.S. by Rita J. Adrosko, Smithsonian Institution.
Nature's Colors: Dyes from Plants by Ida Grae, Macmillan, Inc.
Step-by-Step Weaving by Nell Znamierowski, Golden Press.
Vegetable Dyeing by Alma Lesch, Watson-Guptill Publications.
Vegetable Dyeing by Emma Conley, Penland School of Handcrafts.

Crocheted of wool yarn colored with dye from black-walnut hulls, goldenrod, and other plants, this cushion, entitled "Earthform with Cloves and Rattle," bears mushroomlike forms. It delights all the senses: cloves and a metal container of rice concealed within augment with sound and scent the visual effect.

Participants in a dye workshop in Birmingham, Alabama, many of whom had no prior experience, produced this rainbow of colored yarns in a single day.